CONCILIUM

Religion in the Eighties

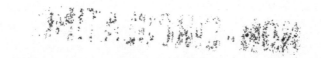

CONCILIUM

Editorial Directors

CONCILIUM

List of Members

Advisory Committee: Fundamental Theology

DIFFERENT THEOLOGIES, COMMON RESPONSIBILITY: BABEL OR PENTECOST?

Edited by
Claude Geffré
Gustavo Gutiérrez
Virgil Elizondo

English Language Editor
Marcus Lefébure

T. & T. CLARK LTD
Edinburgh

February 1984
T. & T. Clark Ltd, 36 George Street, Edinburgh EH2 2LQ
ISBN: 0 567 30051 X

ISSN: 0010-5236

Printed in Scotland by Blackwood, Pillans & Wilson Ltd, Edinburgh

Concilium: Published February, April, June, August, October, December.
Subscriptions 1984: UK £19·00; U.S.A. $40·00; Canada $50·00; Rest of the World
£19·00. Postage and packing included.

CONTENTS

Part III
The Plurality of Theologies as a Theological Problem

Bulletin

Editorial

THE THEME chosen for this first number of the new series of *Concilium* in itself says something about the overall plan of the board of editorial directors. We are trying more and more to offer a platform within the Church to those men and women who are representatives of theologies which are still marginal in relation to the dominant theology. A concrete sign of this intention is the creation of two new sections: *Third World theology* and *Feminist theology*. But contrary to a fear too often voiced, this promotion of different theologies will not be leading us to any kind of slackening, as theologians, of our common responsibility towards the unity of the faith and the unity of the Church.

Any reader wishing to study—without prejudice—the various contributions to this journal will discover two consistently present ideas, notwithstanding the extreme diversity of the authors. First, theological pluralism is only authentic if it is based on a practice of communion and unity. Second, the true 'catholic' unity of the Church is nourished and enriched by a plurality of practices and doctrinal expressions.

In a previous issue devoted to fundamental theology (No 135) we tried to expose a false universality of Christianity which is really nothing but an abstract universality. Unlike the imperialism of the abstract universal, the Christian universal is a universal of gift and mission. In fact it should be called a pascal universal: the Church is ceaselessly exhorted to put to death its special nature in order to be reborn in and from this death . . .

European theology which was, within the Catholic Church, the dominant theology until Vatican II, is called to the same pascal test. Already we can no longer speak of a non-western Third World Church within the great Church. We must now speak of a Third World Church with an originally Western history. Need it be recalled that from the demographic point of view alone, the future of the Church already lies less in the West (Europe and North America) than in Latin America, in Asia and in Africa. This coincides with the end of the colonial era, and following the lines of Vatican II ecclesiology, the local Churches are becoming much more clearly aware of their own cultural identity, and indeed at the very moment when the West is much less confident of its cultural supremacy.

Since the Enlightenment, when the ideology of pluralism was the keynote for modern societies, the Roman Church has reacted by reinforcing even more what might be called a unitary ideology, the typical expression of which was the proclamation of papal infallibility. The anti-pluralist attitude of the Church, directed at first towards the outside world against the various forms of modern liberalism, was exercised more and more within the Church itself. By defining stricter and stricter rules of orthodoxy, the Roman *magisterium* found it more and more difficult to tolerate any doctrinal pluralism.

Today it is difficult to accept the uniformity of a monolithic theology claiming to be universal when it is in fact typically Eurocentric and androcentric, and the rights are claimed of a legitimate pluralism in theology as in Christian practices and liturgical expressions. Even inside the Catholic Church, this pluralism has become a concrete reality, even though it is still scarcely acknowledged in official texts. This pluralism is the expression of the tension between the identical Word of God which concerns all believers and the weight of the historical reality of the Christian communities scattered throughout the world. We cannot appeal to a different Gospel. But the Word of God becomes real only in its reception, which is diverse. Finally, theological pluralism is the consequence of the true absorption into culture of Christianity understood as the prolongation of the mystery of the incarnation as mystery of the conjunction of the particularity of Jesus and the universality of Christ.

Directly or indirectly, *Concilium* has already tackled the question of theological pluralism several times. But here we aim to go one step further. The real goal of this issue is to show that we can and we must finally get out of the false dilemma: either uniformity of theology or shattering of faith. As several articles show on the basis of historical examples, the Church has always been plural, both on the practical and on the doctrinal plane. But it would be irresponsible behaviour to struggle against the monopoly of a Western theology claiming to be universal if at the same time vigilant guard was not kept against a 'balkanisation' of theology delivered up to the pressure of the various national-isms or multiple ideologies. Between these two extremes, either the totalitarianism of unity, or the Babel of disruption, there is nevertheless room for the mystery of Pentecost, as communion in diversity. Under the title 'Different theologies, common responsibility', the sole purpose of this issue is to show that the acceptance of theological pluralism and the division of theological work only strengthen our common responsibility in the mutual recognition of our differences at the service of the unity of the faith. In other words, the way in which each individual theology tries to incarnate the language of the faith in Christ has a prophetic scope for the whole Church. Only if these different voices aroused by the Spirit of the Lord through all time and all space are prepared to listen to one another can the Church accomplish its truly 'catholic' vocation.

In *Part I* we shall try to make a diagnosis both regarding the present situation of theological pluralism in the Church and its most immediate historical causes. Even if the voices of Asia, Africa and Latin America have as yet only feebly made themselves heard, Vatican II represents a break from the dominant pattern of the scholastic theology of the Roman School. This corresponds to the new autonomy of the individual Churches in reaction against Roman centralisation. *P. Eicher* clearly shows how we are witnessing an 'exodus' of theology from the beaten paths of academic theology both in the rich countries of the First World (Germany and the USA) and in the countries of the Third World. But the most decisive phenomenon is not the appearance of new forms of university theology such as transcendental theology, the theology of history or hermen-eutic theology: it is the actual changing of the structures of theology from the fact of its declericalisation. Theology is rooted in the particular experience of a people fighting for its liberation, as is the case of the various theologies of liberation. Or theology is rooted in the historical experience of prolonged marginalisation, as is the case for feminist theology. Finally, the debate on theological pluralism is not only due to particular circumstances; it concerns the very authenticity of a Christian theology which takes seriously the fact that adherence to the same Gospel can be realised only in the diversity of historical situations of the hearers of the Word.

One cannot discuss theological pluralism without bringing in the confrontation of traditional theology with the modernity which began with the Enlightenment. In a few pages *J. B. Metz* manages to state the essentials. The fate of modern theology is of necessity bound to that of the modernity that Western civilisation continues to appeal to. But it is not enough to evoke yet again the crisis theology went through because of the Enlightenment, which meant the end of a religious and metaphysical representation of the world and engendered the now familiar processes of secularisation, emancipation and demythologisa-tion. In a positive dialectical confrontation with the modern world, contemporary theology must face two other crises which signify more or less the end of a rather overweening Eurocentric modernity. First we should sustain the potent memory of Auschwitz which condemns any idealism (including theological idealism), i.e. any system of thought which does not take into account the suffering subjects of history. We should also draw the inferences of the end of the cultural monocentrism of the West and the transition for the Church to polycentrism. The emergence of new theologies in the churches of the Third

World, in particular the theologies of liberation in Latin America, represents an opportunity for any Christian theology to the degree in which they help us to think afresh the unity between the experience of salvation and the experience of liberation and to conceive a new relation between religion and society, between the mystical and the political.

At the dawn of the third millenarium the Church is looking for a unity made up of the communion of the local churches. As president of the Mexican cultural centre of San Antonio, Texas, *Virgil Elizondo* is in a good position to observe the dialogue between the old churches of the northern hemisphere and the young churches of the Third World. In his article he defines the conditions and criteria for an authentic intercultural theological dialogue. We should draw out all the implications of a growing change in the relations between the traditional churches and the young churches. There are no longer mother churches which are universal and daughter churches which are local. There are only sister churches which are all local churches, and it is the task of the theologians to express the faith by remaining faithful to the special genius of their culture, but in dialogue with other theologies.

In *Part II* we have tried to offer a platform to qualified representatives of some specific theologies, asking each author to emphasise the significance for the whole Church of his or her own theology. We begin by hearing the voice of the theology of liberation, the fundamental purpose and prophetic scope of which for any other theology in the Church is plotted for us by *Gustavo Gutiérrez*. And *Elisabeth Schüssler Fiorenza* defines her own feminist theology as a critical theology of liberation. It is a theology which views as its primary task to battle for the liberation of women in society and in the Church. She exposes the limitations of an exclusively male theology which is the accomplice of the still patriarchal structure of the Church and of society. As another example of a specific theology we have given space to *J. A. Bracken* who shows us under what conditions Process philosophy could replace traditional onto-theology in articulating a Christian theology for our times.

We then listen to the challenge of the really different theologies, different in the sense that they are rooted in the historical and cultural experience of a civilisation other than the Western one. *M. Hegba* tells us about the difficulties and opportunities of African theology. We had also asked D. Amalorpavadas to give us an idea of Indian theology, but we did not receive his contribution in the time available. From the point of view of this otherness, it is rather the Western tradition which appears to be a specific tradition even though it was in fact dominant until today. However, it would be quite wrong to identify Western theology with neo-scholastic theology. Especially since the end of the Second World War, European theology has been constantly enriched by ideas taken from Eastern tradition. Hence we tried to include the point of view of an orthodox theologian, but unfortunately his contribution has not reached us.

In *Part III* we take up the fundamental theological thinking on theological pluralism already broached in Part I. We begin with a text by Professor Käsemann who, on the basis of his long familiarity with the texts of the New Testament, tells us how difficult it is to harmonise their different theological traditions. In his view, the unity of the New Testament remains an open question, historically and theologically; and he shows in a striking way how Paul's message which is at the heart of the Gospel was very quickly levelled out and moralised from the beginnings of the Church.

We have already said how difficult it is to get out of the false dilemma of uniformity or fragmentation. *J. M. Tillard*'s article is particularly valuable as he demonstrates on the basis of specific examples how the Church has always been plural and how it has been able to maintain unity of faith in spite of a plurality of liturgical practices and doctrinal expressions. After centuries of monolithism and centralisation, it seems that the Roman Church must start again from zero. In this respect it would have a lot to learn from the Anglican tradition and from its practice of comprehensiveness.

Finally, the last article attempts to show how the plurality of theologies is at the service of a tradition common to all the Church. *N. Lash* thinks that we should break out of the classical mentality and the liberal mentality in order to understand how pluralism contributes to constructing and developing the unity of Christian faith. We should study more profoundly the mystery of the Church, not only as sacrament of the union with God but as sacrament of the unity of all men with one another. If the unity of the Credo is abandoned, its universality is jeopardised. But if the diversity of theologies is done away with, the language of the faith is no longer the expression of this particular history that each section of the people of God is living. In a final Bulletin, *Enrique Dussel* offers us a detailed account of the 'Ecumenical Association of Third World Theologians'. These meetings aim to bridge the gap between a theology of the centre and a theology of the periphery and prepare a future theology which would be truly world-wide.

Such is this issue, made up of a variety of viewpoints. Babel or Pentecost? Even though still tentatively, we have tried to let these different theologies be heard. But we hope that the reader will be sensitive to their polyphony. Our sole ambition is to show that more and more, in the Church of today, it is the mutual recognition of our differences which stimulates our common responsibility as theologians at the service of the same Gospel.

CLAUDE GEFFRÉ
GUSTAVO GUTIÉRREZ
VIRGIL ELIZONDO

Translated by Della Couling

PART I

Diagnosis

Peter Eicher

Pluralism and the Dignity of Theology

'Now we have received not the spirit of the world, but the Spirit which is from God, that we might understand the gifts bestowed on us by God' (1 Cor. 2:12)

1. THE CLOSED SYSTEM

In 1855 the Congregation responsible for the Index compelled Augustin Bonnetty to subscribe to the affirmation that the theological method of Thomas Aquinas, Bonaventure and the later Scholastics 'does not lead to rationalism'.[1] None the less it is a fact that the history of Catholic theology in the four centuries between Trent and Vatican II can be seen essentially as a modern scholasticism which attempts to *rationalise* completely the theology of the High Middle Ages. In psychology 'rationalising' is a symptom of a preoccupation with repressed desires, guilt feelings and traumas under the control of a deeply interiorised censor; in the social sciences 'rationalisation' means the attempt totally to manipulate the cultural milieu, technical information systems and social institutions for the benefit of the increasingly complex administrative sector. In both these senses modern scholasticism became a major instrument in a continuing process of rationalisation within the Church. Whereas in the beginning Trent could still speak in terms of the 'purity of the Gospel itself . . . as the fount of all saving truth and rules of conduct', in the end we find the Church's doctrine of faith, which we believe 'not because of the intrinsic truth of the things . . . but because of the authority of God himself who reveals them':[2] the Church's testimony to the truth of the Gospel has turned into a superior religious knowledge, used for the purposes of domination by a centralising Church administration. In a similarly successful way the attempts of the Scholastics to rationalise the scriptural exegesis of the High Middle Ages were used to parry the fundamental questions raised by the Reformation, oppose the modern critical stance towards religion, and promote the Church's bureaucratisation of the biblical testimony:[3]

In opposing the Reformation, official polemics refused to argue from the hermeneutic basis of scripture, as Luther had demanded in his crucial breakthrough.[4] Instead they became even more attached to the Thomist, Scotist and Ockhamist procedures which the Reformers had rejected as unbiblical. In opposing the claims of modern science and the Enlightenment critique of religion, scholastic apologetics did not work out an integrated interpretation of the soteriological truth of scripture but instead became entrenched in a subtle formalisation of that metaphysical matter which, in its *sacra scriptura*, the High Middle Ages had once developed independently, in open dialogue with contemporary issues. From being essentially a challenge to all times, the Gospel became just one historical event among others and as such needing to be updated. It is well known how the fundamental eschatological tension of Thomas' theology (which ministered in all its parts to the exegesis of scripture) became degraded to the level of an autonomous system of nature and supernature. An abstract concept of 'nature' could meet the (in part) justified demands of Enlightenment scholarship and philosophy; at the same time the independently conceived 'supernatural' order of grace and knowledge seemed to guarantee the superior wisdom and social influence of the Roman Catholic Church. Finally, in opposition to the democratic emancipation of modern man, which had not only demonstrated its legitimacy in the theories of social contract and in the idea of the sovereignty of the people but had achieved *de facto* legality, the hierarchic thought-structures of the High Middle Ages were used improperly but effectively in the defence of an increasingly centralising and absolutist papal Church administration. Thus after Trent the unitary scholastic theology played its part in eliminating the synodal and democratic element of the ancient Church. In short, the scholastic rationalisation of the theology of the High Middle Ages showed itself to be a willing tool in the defensive strategy which characterised the Catholic Church's relationship to the modern world.[5] The Gospel truth of God's free and gracious word, which, if it is to be proclaimed and accepted in faith, presupposes and recognises the formal freedom of all those to whom it is addressed, became instead a religious world-view to be controlled by the Church as if it were a metaphysical law. In a unitary religious metaphysic of this kind, where all theology was *de fide* committed to the system, the only matters worthy or capable of theological discussion were those on the periphery.

Looking back at the period of neo-scholasticism in our search for a self-critical theory of theology, two observations are crucial. First, the *connection* of this European rationalisation of theology with the universal policy of suppression pursued from the end of the fifteenth century by Catholic Spain, Portugal and Italy, attempting not only to exploit economically the civilisations of Central and South America, the coastal regions of Africa and parts of India, but also to make them culturally dependent on their colonisers. The scholastic form of instruction in the Catholic faith became not only the tool of the Inquisition but also the way of legitimising the destruction of non-European civilisation. Secondly, this rationalisation in the direction of a unitary Catholic theology must be seen to be connected with the modern process of de-sacralisation of the world.[6] In scholasticism (primarily that of the Jesuits) the fraternal ethics still operative in the High Middle Ages is changed into a casuistic scheme of life-mastery; the faith that is attuned to prophecy, contemplation and liturgy is reduced to the level of an everyday religious metaphysic; the eschatological vision of a history between creation, redemption and judgment is absorbed into a theology which is both timeless and yet concentrated on the Church in the present; wisdom becomes system, substantial truth becomes functional doctrine, the proclaimed truth becomes a doctrine about the proclamation. In Vatican I we see the results of this one-party approach in its theistic doctrine of God (minus Trinity), its authoritarian and externalised doctrine of revelation and faith (minus a theology of the word of God), and its positivistic ecclesiology of the *magisterium* (minus the dimensions of christology and pneumatology). All the attempts, variously suppressed, to bring about a renewal of modern Catholic theology (historico-critical exegesis, Enlightenment theology, theology of history, ecumenism) had to lie hidden below the ashes of time until, in the context of Vatican II, a mature theological account of faith arrived, fanning them into flame once more.

2. THE CAUTIOUS OPENING

Laboriously, circuitously, the Catholic Church's authorities in the twentieth century have found their way back to more *indirect* recognition of those theologies which, instead of working with a doctrine already sanctioned by the Church, react creatively and responsibly in their own way to the biblical witness to God's living word. But it has been a hard road: for even at Vatican II the recognition in principle of theology's own special task arose not from an insight into its irreplaceable dignity as a truth-medium, but from the realisation that its relative freedom was necessary if the Church's teaching was to be defended. For instance, the papal *magisterium* opposed the idea of human rights, religious freedom and the right of public opinion until the Church itself was compelled to embrace them in order to survive in Fascist and Stalinist regimes. But this granting of a relative theological diversity in the Catholic Church was *indirect*: Church authorities were concerned not so much with the *pluriformity of historical responses* to God's word as with their own *anxiety about the unity* of a world Church which, since the Second World War, had been diversifying in a revolutionary manner:

— Only after the Christian churches had been brought closer to one another by the grievous effects of the war and an industrial society which was atheistic as a matter of course, did the Catholic Church accept the biblical witness of God's own word as both the foundation and the criterion of all church theologies (see *Dei Verbum* 24; *Presb. ord.* 19); only then did it grant a 'proper freedom' to the various theological disciplines (*Unit. red.* 4).

— Right up to the final consolidation of the Soviet regime, Vatican diplomacy (Benedict XV, 1914-1922, and Pius XI, 1922-1939) had hoped to take advantage of the separation of the Orthodox Church and the Tsarist State (achieved by the October Revolution of 1917) and win Eastern Christians for the papal and Roman Church.[7] It was not until the Stalinist terror, with its considerably intensified persecution of the Church which made no distinction between the Russian Orthodox and the Roman Catholic Church, i.e., not until 1929 at the latest, that the Latin Church came to a deeper appreciation of Eastern patristic theology, acknowledging it as a common tradition of biblical interpretation (see LG 23; *Unit. red.* 14) capable of going beyond the scholastic limits of the 'universal' Church. Today it is precisely the efforts towards unity, in the face of the *de facto* pluralism of Christendom, which are leading to an inner expansion of Roman Catholic theology.

— Following the widespread loss of currency of all religious metaphysics, Church authorities, if they wished to pursue their claims to a world-view, had to look ultimately for a new connection between the witness of faith and the scientific world. Now the relative autonomy of theology becomes a means of applying the Gospel, interpreted by the Church, to a context which is structurally god-less. Thus the Church urges theologians not only to undertake 'research' but also 'not to lose contact with their own times' (*Gaudium et spes* 62). As the disciplinary procedures at all levels of theology and proclamation have since shown, this was still not a recognition in principle of theology's dignity as a truth-medium, but an acknowledgment of its relative usefulness in support of official Church teaching existing independently of it. So too John Paul II admits that theology has an autonomous *function* vis-à-vis the *magisterium*, but in the same breath he denies that the scriptural truth arrived at by theology has any binding influence upon the decisions of the *magisterium* itself.[8]

— With regard to theological 'pluralism' in the Church, the decisive development at Vatican II was that the cultural richness of those countries which Europe had oppressed by its colonialism, politics, even by its missionising and hence its theology, could no longer be absorbed into the categories of the Roman, scholastic, rational power-machine: all the conciliar decrees prepared by the Roman school were simply swept aside by the spirit of the universal Church. All the same, there was little real listening to the voices of Asia, Africa and Latin America at the Council; the dominant model in the minds of the Council Fathers was still that of extending and adapting the traditional theology to the spirit and distinctive quality of every culture. Yet the door to a perception of a new theology which would be in no way scholastic had been opened a fraction. Once the Council, in opposition to Roman centralism, had affirmed the relative autonomy of the episcopal sees and regional churches, it could also be expected that the diverse theologies of these churches would be recognised as a pluriform language expressing the one truth of faith.

3. THE EXODUS FROM ACADEMIC THEOLOGY

Since theology neither needs nor can be anything other than the interpretation of scripture for the Church's life in society, it is in a constant tension between the word of God proclaimed in the Bible and the historical reality of the Christian communities. Contemporaries may feel that their times show nothing but confusion, later historical reflection can reveal the outlines of an intelligible development. In the short period since the Second World War a twofold development can be traced in Catholic theology, which sheds light on the significance of the current luxuriant wealth of theologies.

The first line can be called 'catching up with modernity'. It characterises academic theology in the rich industrial centres of Germany and the USA in particular. It is especially noticeable in exegesis, which for the most part simply repeats all the results of the historico-critical method, worked out for the last three hundred years in the Protestant churches, though largely without appreciating the cul-de-sac into which the 'history of religions' school had ultimately led. At the same time systematic theology has been endeavouring to integrate our modern inheritance, piece by piece, into the old cosmos of Catholic consciousness: transcendental theology connects scholasticism with modern metaphysics up to Kant and Fichte, the phenomenological theology of glory and the theology of history are involved with Idealist and late Kantian material, theological hermeneutics and the historical school continue the work of nineteenth century historicism and hermeneutics,[9] etc. But all these theologies remain within the university education establishment, which is concerned with the consensus of scholars about the doctrine itself and not with the actual consciousness of the people to whom it is addressed. We need hardly say how much the Catholic theologies are indebted to the great edifice of Protestant theology. But the fundamental change taking place today in Catholic theology is not the discovery of yet another academic theology, but the transformation of the basic structures of theology itself. Previously it was the trained, masculine and priestly specialist who was regarded as theologically competent; now, over the whole world, a theological emancipation of the whole people is taking place: every Christian who, in his own community, is able to communicate the claims of the Gospel as they impinge on that situation, is theologically competent. Theology is becoming the everyday practice of prophecy. Published 'liberation theology' for the most part provides only an academic echo of what is going on. Whereas academic reflection is primarily concerned with the widest possible, most universal communication, the people's theology is concerned with the particular, the unique witness. From the point of view of the people's theology, academic theology seems to be a part of that system of domination which is co-responsible for its economic, political and intellectual misery. Thus, as far as the centres of economic and political power are concerned, the distinctions drawn by the theology of the 'basic communities' are quite different from those arising from the cultural background of academic reflection. Hence feminist theology's critique of the masculine, rational dominance reveals an alienation in the documents of faith themselves such as no male theologian would have dreamt of contemplating, and lay theology, having been continually subordinated to priestly theology, is particularly sensitive to the clerical disenfranchisement of the faithful. In this situation, political theology endeavours to put the faithful's grassroots critique in touch with the Church's academic élite, thus facilitating solidarity in the practice of an eschatologically orientated faith.

Is all this to be seen and substantiated in terms of 'theological pluralism'? Or does this pluriformity call for quite a different view of the dignity of theology in the Church?

4. WHAT IS 'PLURALISM'?

It does not mean simply any multiplicity of groups, theories and interests. It refers to a group of theorists which describe and justify those liberal democracies which are organised economically according to free market principles and politically according to the multi-party system representing a sovereign people.[10] As far as middle-class society is concerned, the theory of 'pluralism' legitimises the economic, social and political competition of groups within the State which recognise each other as having equal rights and keep an eye on each other in view of common interests and agreements. Seen historically, this liberal ideal of a social *consent* on the basis of the greatest possible opportunity for *dissent* presupposes the development of an autonomous middle class within the modern national States.[11]

But the theory of 'pluralism' not only describes in a non-judgmental way the struggle for 'life, liberty and the pursuit of happiness' which is constitutive of middle-class society. It also defends as normative the specific freedoms of the open society: tolerance towards all world-views (except the anti-pluralist); the principle of achievement, which commends to each, equally, the acquisition of political, economic and social power (in fact legitimising the strong and putting the weaker at a disadvantage); the strong encouragement to solve conflicts by compromise and public discussion (which is dominated by those most adept at winning battles); and the right to distinctness within a federative system (which so far is not compatible with solidarity shown to weaker groups and regions). As far as pluralism in the Church is concerned, feared by many and longed for by many others, it is illuminating to pinpoint the internal difficulties of the individual theorems:

Since Alexis de Tocqueville's justification of democracy in America,[12] American theories of pluralism, unlike the liberal theories of the State in Europe, did not have to make headway against an authoritarian and feudal society, but against the inhumane consequences of their own system. In *laissez-faire liberalism* the model of a supposedly free market economy, which only needed the State as the regulator of its own interests, inevitably led to the political dominance of strong cartels which destroy this very principle of the freedom of all citizens to compete. Consequently the *corporative pluralism* which was critical of this competitive struggle wanted to see the institutionalisation of permanent interest-groups which would also be able to represent politically those groups that were disadvantaged. Up to now, however, it too has not been able to inhibit the egoism of pressure-groups and give a voice to those oppressed in the competition process and to those groups which are not capable of standing up for themselves in the struggle. So, in the end, there developed the concept of the 'open pluralism' (Kelso)[13] which is characteristic of the present situation. Here it is the powerful State itself (Congress, Supreme Court, President) which should protect the interests of marginal groups—as if government officers in the pluralist State did not by definition represent the interests of powerful groups. It is not hard to imagine what an effect, in the long run, these models of competition would have on the Church's internal development . . . The inner contradiction of the theories of pluralism can be seen in the case of neo-liberal political theory in West Germany: here the free play of forces can only be fostered on the basis of *fundamental values* prescribed in the Constitution and promoted by a strong *government*, which exclude the enemies of pluralism themselves from competition for power.[14] Apparently democracy cannot be built on pluralism but only on a sharing of fundamental values by consensus.

The most influential theory of the social sciences at the present time (see Jürgen Habermas) corresponds to the pluralist view of post-war German society: all scientific and scholarly work is understood in terms of communication, which must assert itself, against competition, among the community of scholars by means of argument.[15] Here, theories are valid so long as they are not refuted by a consensus of scholars. While it is true that all participants in the scientific discussion are required to show both the willingness and the ability to embrace truth and fairness, this theory likewise leads to the dilemma of all theories of pluralism. It cannot show how any actual consensus can be true, nor can it formulate universal criteria for a successful agreement. Consequently the pluralist theory of knowledge is unable to recognise the validity of theological arguments, because it considers the truth of faith to which theology refers to be obsolete as a result of evolution. It no longer has public validity. Here we see the fulfilment of a view which began in the Enlightenment in the context of the religious wars which threatened the existence of States: religion's dogmatic content is neutralised in the interests of public life and action. All ideas of faith are optional in the pluralist State; therefore faith itself can only be 'verified' pragmatically, i.e., by its concrete action.

If theology is not to misunderstand itself fundamentally, it must not seek to justify its own truth in terms of the pluralist competition for validity and public influence, nor must it accept the pragmatic view that its theoretical statements are purely optional. Pluralism certainly can show us how difficult it is to hold together freedom and truth, multiplicity and unity, tolerance and respect for the less powerful voice. Theology can only arrive at this liberating pluriformity of the one truth if it is always conscious, both within the Church and in the face of society, of the dignity of its special theme: the dignity of the word of God which has become history. Since this one word looks for a manifold response to its redeeming truth, theology must minister to it in a whole variety of ways. But since its subject matter is *this one* truth, theology is not at the mercy of the pluralist competition which dominates science and public opinion. The pluriform theologies, which are to be respected as such by the Church's leaders, are based solely on the activity of the word of God attested in the Bible; as a result they must be critical of the pluralist concept of truth.

5. AUTHORITY OF DOCTRINE

The Gospel contained in both Old and New Testaments does not call for blind submission but for 'obedience to the truth' (1 Pet. 1:22). This invitation to life by the power of God's living word must not be understood, however, as a summons to a philosophic stance, and even less as a prophetic announcement of the autonomy of science. For a life of this kind is not based on a sense of security, won through argument, amid the myriad offerings of human wisdom; rather it is due solely to the power of the word of God which calls and invites us: 'You have been born anew, not of perishable seed but of imperishable, through the living and abiding word of God' (1 Pet. 1:23). A theology which is grounded on this biblical witness to God's active word will be reminded of its obedience to the truth in three ways:
— In the real context of history the proclamation of God's righteous, merciful and faithful Gospel makes it clear how far all human reason is imprisoned in self-interest by the powers of this age and hence by disobedience to God's own glory (see Rom. 1:18-24). 'But the scripture,' writes Paul himself, 'consigned all things to sin' (Gal. 3:22;

see Rom. 11:32). According to this, theology cannot base itself on a consensus among the multiplicity of ideas of God in the history of religions; by contrast, it begins with the 'word of reconciliation': 'All this is from God, who through Christ reconciled us to himself and gave us the ministry of reconciliation' (2 Cor. 5:18). Since all theologies confess their faith in the redemption, ultimately they can only present their wisdom to the public in the form of a plea—'be reconciled to God' (2 Cor. 5:20) and in the form of gratitude: 'so that as grace extends to more and more people it may increase thanksgiving, to the glory of God' (2 Cor. 4:15). By pleading for forgiveness and giving thanks for reconciliation we strike at the root of the ill-conceived dispute about which is the right theology: *this* process of communication, by faith, brings about the proper unity of truth in the Church.

— In speaking of God's activity, as scripture does, theology is not committing itself to the mythological ideas according to which God intervenes in mundane events by empirical causality. It is rather that God operates through his word, creatively, in judgment, in promise, in redemption. Given, however, that God never acts apart from his word, he himself is only experienced when he is heard and acknowledged in his word. What was true of the invisible word of God in the OT Gospel applies all the more to the proclamation of the Word-made-man: it is the hearing, acknowledging and following of the preached Jesus which enables those who have been created anew in the spirit of the word of Christ to act in faith: 'but whoever keeps his word, in him truly love for God is perfected. By this we may be sure that we are in him: he who says he abides in him ought to walk in the same way in which he walked' (1 John 2:5f). But the word which, by the spirit which indwells it, guides the actions of the community of faith, is not uttered over the heads of the various communities and individuals; nor can it achieve expression apart from their own thoughts and conceptions. Just as, if the word is to be perceived, it needs the manifest faith-commitment of the community which is being reconciled by it, so each individual in this community needs his own independent recognition of its truth if he is to believe.

— The Gospel itself distinguishes between this *prophetic witness* to God's Word-made-man and the *teaching* concerning this Word.[16] True, the missionary *proclamation* (kerygma) is never separated from the *teaching* (didaskalia) which is distinct from it, but there is an increasing differentiation of these two basic community functions: as early as Paul, who saw himself not only as an apostle and prophet but evidently as a teacher as well (see Rom. 6:17; 16:17), we find a distinction between the various gifts of the Spirit with regard to teaching—i.e., the 'utterance of wisdom' and the 'utterance of knowledge' and the 'ability to distinguish between spirits' (1 Cor. 12:8, 10)—and the charisms of prophecy, healing and tongues. It is the one Spirit who gives to each in his own way for the good of all (1 Cor. 12:7, 11). This already implies not only that the one Spirit of Jesus Christ operates and is conceived in very diverse ways, but also that, within the pluriform community, there is a single 'analogy of faith' (Rom. 12:6), i.e., a *single* rule of faith, which is to be taught. It is this which enables the Spirit of Christ to be distinguished from the wisdom of this world. When Matthew makes it clear to the teachers of his community that they are not to be called 'Rabbi', 'for you have one teacher, and you are all brethren' (Matt. 23:8), we can see the concern exercised to preserve the correct teaching of the 'one teacher' in the community. The four gospels (twenty years after the *corpus paulinum*, be it noted) themselves show the concern for the *one* true doctrine in its pluriform effects and expressions. The '*one* teacher' speaks in *many* ways, because he will not short-circuit the minds and hearts of the faithful in his desire to lead them to their life's truth in fellowship with God: he waits for the *consent* of their faith. But this has to take place in the extremely varied situations of those who hear the word. The Gospel is given by God, but at the same time it has to reach man. And though it is given, not manipulable, it is encountered by men who exhibit the extremes of diversity within human history. The *one* teaching of the Gospel can only be *Gospel* teaching if it reflects this multiplicity.

6. THE FREEDOM OF THEOLOGY

God's word has a dignity of its own. Where it becomes the object of technical research or an instrument used for extraneous purposes by the Church or society, it ceases to be the way which is the truth and the life (see John 14:6f). Since God's word, revealed to faith in the testimony of scripture, imparts a share in his own life to all who recognise it, it can never be made into a means for particular ends: here instrumental reason (*uti*) is inappropriate; God's word calls for joy in the truth (*frui*), which also involves the blessed destiny of being persecuted for the sake of this truth (see Matt. 5:10). Theology cannot surrender the self-respect which accords with the dignity of its subject at any price, neither for academic respectability, society, nor the Church.

— We must distinguish in principle between responsibility for leadership of the community and the pastoral teaching office, on the one hand, and the charism of theology, on the other. For it is one thing to present arguments in favour of the *truth* of faith and another to decide whether the truth, thus arrived at, can *achieve consensus* in the community of faith. It is one thing to submit the content of the received faith of the Church to theological criticism to see whether it corresponds to the truth of God's word, and another to proclaim and teach the inherited faith. Theology cannot be commanded or produced to order: it is totally charisma, a free gift of the Spirit. Ultimately all the Church's theologian can do is perceive it in its integrity. Disciplinary measures by Church authorities cannot extinguish this particular charism, but they can restrict its influence on the community.

— Theology owes its dignity not only to its subject but also to its own responsibility as a science. Even if today, after almost a century of research, there is no material consensus as to what constitutes a scholarly discipline, we can cite formal traits common to all scholarly activity. Central to all is the repudiation of any administrative compulsion: scientific statements and techniques can only be achieved or altered as a result of reasoning, never through external pressure. Even the consensus which scholars look for and which the teaching office crystallises, cannot be the formal basis of scientific truth; rather it is the truth-intention which is the presupposition for any consensus. Whether 'truth' is seen ontologically, pragmatically or in terms of communication theory, ultimately the only scientific reason for assenting to it is insight into the truth of statements. Truth is expected of theology. It must not surrender what thus belongs to its very being; in fact theology lives by *participation* in the truth that is revealed eschatologically to faith. The truth-claim recognises no institutional frontiers: of its very nature it seeks to broadcast itself limitlessly. The sciences do the same, not only to bring their influence to bear, but because their own fallibility needs constant revision of statements. Thus, scientifically speaking, a proposition cannot be true unless it is formulated in such a way as to be falsifiable. There is no reason to exclude theology from this scientific dignity of truth; on the contrary: its subject-matter, God's word, likewise tolerates no institutional interference, nor does it depend on consensus; it summons those who hear to come to a consensus on the basis of the *truth* of faith of God's word. However taboo the recourse to public opinion may still be in the Catholic Church, the fact remains that the avoidance of public discussion never speaks for the truth; it only indicates fear of it.

— It is unworthy of theology to demand tolerance of society and of Church authorities for itself alone. If it is prepared to make room for the word of God, which speaks for itself, it will have to minister to the freedom of all, including those who, according to their own lights, misunderstand this word or feel obliged to offer vehement criticism of

it. (Catholics who campaign in principle against Marxists' freedom to teach are in fact undermining the presuppositions of their own action.) In the struggle for the truth of the Gospel the only stance which befits the dignity of theology is that of publicly presented argument, relying on the self-evident truth of the sovereign word of God.
— Finally, 'many wonder why there are so many novelties in the Church of God. Why have so many groups come about within it?' Anselm von Havelberg gave an answer to this question in 1145 which is worth listening to with regard to today's plurality of academic (and totally unacademic) forms of theology: 'The body of the Church, which is truly animated by the Holy Spirit . . . remains always united in one faith, but it manifests a multiplicity of forms on account of the great diversity of life within it'.[17] About this 'multiplici vivendi varietas' exhibited in the profusion of grassroots theologies, the academics of the 'one theology' school still have everything to learn. Not only Church authorities, but theologies too are 'semper reformanda'.

Translated by Graham Harrison

Notes

1. DS 2814.
2. See DS 1501 and 1526 with DS 3008.
3. See P. Eicher *Offenbarung—Prinzip neuzeitlicher Theologie* (Munich 1977) pp. 73-164, 487-547; *id.*, *Theologie, Eine Einführung in das Studium* (Munich 1980) pp. 90-102, 178-183—*La théologie comme science pratique* (Paris 1982) pp. 105-120, 212-218.
4. See H. O. Pesch *Hinführung zu Luther* (Mainz 1982) pp. 38, 48-79.
5. See K. Gabriel, F. X. Kaufmann *Zur Soziologie des Katholizismus* (Mainz 1980); P. Eicher 'Von den Schwierigkeiten bürgerlicher Theologie mit den katholischen Kirchenstrukturen' in *Theologie in Freiheit und Verantwortung* ed. K. Rahner, H. Fries (Munich 1981) pp. 96-137.
6. See M. Weber *Gesammelte Aufsätze zur Religionssoziologie I* (Tübingen ⁶1972) pp. 536-573; J. B. Metz *Glaube in Geschichte und Gesellschaft* (Mainz 1978); P. Eicher *Bürgerliche Religion. Eine theologische Kritik* (Munich 1983).
7. See H. Stehle *Die Ostpolitik des Vatikans, 1917-1975* (Munich 1975).
8. On the recognition of theology's relative autonomy, see AAS LXXIII (1981) No. 1, p. 100; on his address to the International Theological Commission, see *Oss. Rom.* 7.10.81.
9. Survey in e.g. P. Eicher *Theologie* pp. 169-210; on the continuation of this hermeneutics, see esp. C. Geffré *Le Christianisme au risque de l'interpretation* (Paris 1983).
10. For an introduction, see J. Wahl *The Pluralistic Philosophies of England and America* (London 1925); H. Kariel *The Decline of American Pluralism* (Stanford 1961); K. Rahner *Theological Investigations* VI, pp. 3ff, 21ff, 31ff; X, p. 318ff; XI, p. 3ff; XII, p. 202ff; *Die Einheit des Glaubens und der theologische Pluralismus* ed. International Theological Commission (Einsiedeln 1973); H. Kremendahl *Pluralismustheorie in Deutschland* (Leverkusen 1977); G. Lindgens *Katholische Kirche und moderner Pluralismus* (Stuttgart 1980); *Pluralismus, Grundlegung und Diskussion* ed. H. Oberreuter (Opladen 1980).
11. On the concept of the middle-class society, see M. Riedel 'Gesellschaft, bürgerliche' in *Geschichtliche Grundbegriffe II* (Stuttgart 1973) pp. 719-800: *Concilium* 125 (1979); W. Conze 'Bürgertum, Neuzeit' in *Theologische Realenzyklopadie VII* (Berlin, New York 1980) pp. 346-354; W. Müller 'Bürgertum und Christentum' in *Christlicher Glaube in moderner Gesellschaft 19* (Freiburg, Basle, Vienna 1982) pp. 5-58; P. Eicher *Bürgerliche Religion* (see note 6).
12. See W. Steffani 'Vom Pluralismus zum Neopluralismus' in H. Oberreuter (see note 10) pp. 37-108, 41f.

13. W. A. Kelso *American Democratic Theory—Pluralism and its Critics* (Westport, Conn. and London 1978) concludes: 'The pluralistic interplay of groups may not be self-sustaining, but if it is properly regulated, it may be far superior to the alternatives . . .' (p. 270).

14. Conservative criticism is also applied at this point to the liberal Christian theory of pluralism; see B. V. Greiff 'Pluralismustheorie und Status quo, Kritik an A. Schwan' in *Merkur 33* (1979) pp. 1063-1077; A. Schwan 'Pluralismus und Wahrheit' in *Christlicher Glaube in moderner Gesellschaft 18* (Freiburg, Basle, Vienna 1981) pp. 143-211.

15. See H. Peukert *Wissenschaftstheorie-Handlungstheorie-Fundamentale Theologie* (Frankfurt ²1978); J. Habermas *Theorie des kommunikativen Handelns* 2 vols (Frankfurt 1981); for a theological critique see P. Eicher *Bürgerliche Religion* (see note 6) Studie VII.

16. See H. Schürmann *Orientierungen am Neuen Testament* (Düsseldorf 1978) pp. 116-156; F. Hahn 'Urchristliche Lehre und neutestamentliche Theologie' in *Die Theologie und das Lehramt* ed. W. Kern (Freiburg, Basle, Vienna 1982) pp. 63-115.

17. 'Solent plerique mirari et in quaestionen ponere . . . Quare tot novitates in Ecclesia Dei fiunt? Quare tot ordines in ea surgunt?' (Dialogi I, PL 188, 1141C). His reply to the question of the multiplicity of new orders is a pneumatological one: 'Quod unum corpus Ecclesiae uno Spiritu Sancto regitur et gubernatur . . . Verum hoc corpus Ecclesiae Spiritu Sancto vivificatum . . . semper unum una fide, sed multiformiter distinctum multiplici vivendi varietate' (PL 188, 1143D-1144C); see Y. Congar 'Die Lehre von der Kirche' in *Handbuch der Dogmengeschichte III, 3c* (Freiburg, Basle, Vienna 1971) p. 81.

Johann-Baptist Metz

Theology in the Modern Age, and before its End

ANYONE WHO tries to determine the fate of theology with regard to the modern age cannot just produce a partial synopsis of the history of theology: rather, he or she must tackle some of the theology of history.

(1) To begin with, even in theology we have moved on a long way from working with the traditional pattern of antiquity, the middle ages, and modern times as a way of dividing up the history of theology and the Church. At the very least the concept of modern times is taken in a much more differentiated way. The epoch labelled as the modern age no longer simply begins with the religious and secular divides of the sixteenth century and what led up to them, but with the processes of the Enlightenment which have had persistent effects on the fields of the sciences and intellectual inquiry and of political life (thanks to the French and American revolutions)—and these effects extend to the way theology sees itself. This Enlightenment is not simply a historical process but something that is still present, especially when two considerations are borne in mind. First, even socialism sees itself as the child and heir of the Enlightenment, and hence the two major ideological blocs in the world today interpret themselves as dependent on the Enlightenment—even if for the socialist revolution the problem remains that it itself began in a pre-bourgeois and indeed feudalistic society and so far has only been able to establish itself successfully in such societies. Secondly, it should not be overlooked that even the fundamental crises of the Enlightenment which have for example led to the formulation of the 'dialectic of the Enlightenment' are still understood as aspects of these very processes of Enlightenment.

(2) These processes of Enlightenment by which the modern age continues to be defined and determined are to be regarded as processes strictly centred on the West and Europe, if for the moment we take Europe and North America together. Mex Weber coined the term 'occidental rationality' to describe them, something which has meanwhile arrived at a kind of world domination by means of the spread of technology and the ideologies contained within it as well as by means of the instrumental reason of the sciences.

(3) These processes have led to a fundamental crisis of Christian theology. Universally recognised labels for this are the processes of secularisation and of emancipation (of classes and races, and, as is now emerging, of women), of demythologisation, etc. The attempt to grapple with these crises at their roots and to digest them theologically

13

has dissolved the classical unity of theology and led to a variety of forms for theology's attempt to give an account of the hope that is in us. I shall list some crises coming to terms with which radically affects the shape of doing theology.

(a) First of all there is the disintegration of the religious and metaphysical images of the world in these processes of the Enlightenment. The crisis of theology occasioned by this disintegration applies also to the Reformation and its theologies, since the Reformation took place within the framework of an all-embracing Christian understanding of the world. This disintegration brought to an end the stage of theology's cognitive innocence. Since then theology must grapple with the questioning of its historical innonence by the concentration on historical data and development and of its social innocence by the bourgeois and Marxist versions of the critique of ideology. No longer can it displace the questions connected with this from the centre to the apologetic fringes of theology and continue undisturbed with the enterprise of theology, protected by this kind of apologetics. The *logos* of theology is itself affected by this crisis. It cannot withdraw from these questionings to a completely secure metaphysical foundation. Historical as well as social questions penetrate to the core of theology and demand an extremely differentiated treatment that can no longer be provided by the individual theological practitioner. Theological learning is from now on conducted in a plural community of communication—or else it comes to nothing or, what ultimately comes to the same thing, falls back into the classical systemisation. Coming to terms with these crises thus compelled an internal pluralisation of theological initiatives, leading for example to the initiatives of what is termed liberal theology concerned especially with the problems of historicism, the initiatives of a dialectical theology trying to escape from the identification of bourgeois and Messianic religion, and the initiatives of recent political theologies which have above all sought to tackle the problems which arise from a post-idealist critique of religion and which for their part fight against the identification of Christianity with the political religions of enlightened societies or the myths that provide them with legitimacy (civil religion, bourgeois religion).

(b) The processes of the Enlightenment mean that theology itself is threatened by a twofold reduction which at the same time presents something like a permanent constitutional crisis for theology. In the first place we can talk of a privatistic reduction of theology in which the *logos* of theology is entirely concentrated on religion as a private affair and thus is in danger of losing continuity with the Messianic cause of Christianity. On the other hand, one can obviously talk of the danger of a rationalistic reduction of theology, in other words of a withering of the imagination, a radical renunciation of symbolism and mythology under the excessive cognitive pressure of the abstract modern world of the sciences. Of course the processes of the Enlightenment do not mean either that society has been completely secularised or that religion and with it theology completely privatised. Indeed, one of theology's tasks in the criticism of society involved in the processes of the Enlightenment is to unmask the idea of a completely secularised society and in this sense one that has been completely rationalised as the specific myth which a non-dialectical setting up of Enlightenment as an absolute always produces. This task of criticising society that falls to theology will of course turn out differently according to the different political cultures that theology is confronted with.[1]

(c) The processes of the Enlightenment, especially in the various forms of the critique of ideology, have also forced on theology in a new way the question of who does theology, where it is done and the interests of those involved. Through the development of the dialectic of theory and practice theology has been thrown back on to the practical foundation of its wisdom and its formation of theories. This point of view has far-reaching consequences. The question arises whether theology can see itself solely within the framework of the existing ecclesiastical and social division of labour, in other words in practice theology as part of academic education taught by professional theologians at institutions like universities and seminaries established by secular society and the Church. At present another form is emerging alongside this (indispensable) form of doing theology. Not without ambiguity this is labelled grassroots theology, and an initial report on it was given in volume 5 of 1978 of this journal. Productive examples can above all be found in the theologies of liberation, as well as in the form of the Black theologies and in the initiatives of feminist theology.

(*d*) To this must be added the fact that the profound and indeed catastrophic crises which emerge in the process of Enlightenment (and which may be due to its being set up as an absolute in an undialectical way) have led to an additional crises of theology. Here I would simply refer to the catastrophe of Auschwitz. If theology wants to remain itself by not turning its back on such catastrophes and does not wish to betray its historical responsibility, then it must regard as finished that form of theological idealism not centred on a particular agent with which German theology has supplied the Christian world. A theology aware of such catastrophes can no longer be a theology locked into a concept of a system but must become one locked into a concept of the active agent, and one with a practical foundation. In the face of such catastrophes theology is directed from history in the singular to histories of suffering in the plural. These can never be explained in an idealistic fashion but merely recalled with a practical purpose. In this sense theology must become its own critique of ideology: it must learn to see through the high content of apathy of theological idealism and to unmask its lack of sensitivity for the discontinuous character of historical and political catastrophes. Once again this leads precisely to giving a theological vindication of the Gospel in the face of the modern age and its catastrophes, and doing this in the framework of an internal theological pluralism.

(4) Attention should be drawn to a specifically Catholic dilemma with regard to the modern age and the processes of scientific and political Enlightenment that have taken place in it. It is well known that the Catholic Church and the main stream of its theology has taken up a more or less defensive attitude to the European history of the modern age. Rather than playing a genuinely creative role in the modern age's history of freedom, and particularly in the processes of bourgeois and post-bourgeois Enlightenment, it has for the most part opposed this. What have been termed the Catholic ages within the modern age, and particularly since the Enlightenment, have essentially always been 'anti' ages: the age of the counter-reformation, the age of the counter-Enlightenment, the age of the counter-revolution, the age of political restoration and the romantic movement. In this one can of course see considerable awareness of the internal contradictions of this European modern age and its history of freedom, one can indeed recognise at least a latent feeling for its internal dialectic. But must one not also see historical omissions which in fact have made it so difficult for the Catholic Church and its theology to deal creatively with the history of religion and the history of freedom? Is it merely by accident that Catholics are regarded as notorious late developers and as it were as dyslexics in the school of freedom? How can the dilemma indicated here be overcome? Can Catholics and Catholic theology appeal to a history of freedom which was fought and suffered for not only without them but to a considerable extent against them? Is there any credible way of overcoming this dilemma which affects both the credibility of theology and its applicability in practice?

(5) The prospect I shall try to introduce in the considerations that follow may seem questionable to many in view of the problems that have accumulated. It can even appear today like a devious attempt to escape from theology's difficulties and dilemmas in face of the modern age. I myself see in it an authentic way for the Church and theology to follow. I would not mention it if it did not already exist in hints and beginnings—in the life of the Church, in the changes taking place in theology. It is a question of whether the profoundly European-centred modern age has not been overcome in embryo for the Church and for theology, and whether these new ways do not also indicate a solution for

the dilemma that has been indicated and an inspiration for coping creatively with the demands made on theology by the modern age.

We shall disregard the fact that there is talk of such an 'end' in the cultural and political field. In the cultural field which is my background there is in any case an abundance of such indications of an end,[2] and recently the question of a new relationship between mythology and modernity has cropped up among us again.[3] I admit that, in view of the recent history of my country, I am not a little frightened by enthusiasm for the idea of myth (in the non-theological sphere). My starting point is that myth is used here to describe that uncomprehended totality of a revolutionary transformation in thought and attitude with which we are continually confronted by the global problems that have meanwhile become problems of everyday life: the relationship between rich and poor in this world, the ecological question, and underlying everything the question of peace. Talking of myth and modernity remains acceptable if myth does not stand here for a dangerous regressive de-differentiation of all these vital questions but for awareness of a turning-point which in what follows I can only indicate in the life of the Church and of theology.

(a) Today, for example, we must start from the fact that the Church no longer simply 'has' a third world Church outside Europe but that it 'is' a third world Church with its origins and its history in the West and Europe. To put it another way, the Church today is in transition from what culturally is a more or less monocentric Church of Europe and North America to a culturally polycentric universal Church. In this sense it stands at the end and watershed of a modern age that is characterised in exclusively Eurocentric terms. And this is of great importance not just for the life of the Church but for the fate of theology, since the Church's social history affects the intellectual history of theology.[4]

In order to make the theological importance of this new situation clear, I would like to divide the history of the Church and of theology so far into three epochs:[5] the epoch of Jewish Christianity, relatively short in terms of years but fundamental for the identity of the Church and of theology; then the very long epoch within a single culture, even if one with many different strands, in other words the epoch of Hellenism and European culture and civilisation up to our own days; and finally the epoch of a culturally polycentric genuinely universal Church whose first hints and beginnings showed them-selves at Vatican II. The end of cultural monocentrism does not mean its dissolution into an arbitrary contextual pluralism which enables Western and European theology to maintain itself unscathed overagainst these non-European cultures and churches. Embedded in this cultural polycentrism is the history of the Church's Western origins, which in practice was also always a history of guilt (with regard to the non-European cultures). But now it is a question of mutual inspiration and mutual creative assimilation.

(b) In putting these ideas forward I must of course presuppose a great deal which cannot be expounded and demonstrated in detail here: for example, the fact that in the contemporary world such a cultural polycentrism does in fact (still) exist, in other words that it has not already been replaced in embryo by that secular Europeanisation of the world that we call technology or technological civilisation and thus by the universal domination of occidental rationality—in which of course far more of Europe's history, anthropology and politics are bidden than the technocrats of all shades of opinion would have us believe. Then we must presuppose the view strongly represented in modern theories of culture,[6] that there is something like a mutually inspiring creative assimilation of different cultures.

If nevertheless this broad diagnosis remains acceptable as a hypothesis in the theology of history, this has far-reaching consequences for the questions raised here. To elucidate this I shall confine myself in this context exclusively with the relationship with the Latin American church. The objection could perhaps be raised that this is not a suitable example to illustrate ecclesiastical and theological polycentrism in what one might term the post-modern age because the cultures of Latin America have as it were been projected across the Atlantic from Europe. But if we start from the idea that in Latin America's religious and political cultures we are not just faced with a projection of Europe, then consideration of the Church and the theology of these countries is full of promise. Mutual inspiration and creative assimilation between individual cultural spheres only occurs when they are not totally alien and unrelated to each other.

(*c*) In fact in this cultural sphere we meet an ecclesiastical and theological life from which, within the culturally polycentric educational framework of the one Church, we can obtain impulses for grappling creatively with those problems and for overcoming that Catholic dilemma that I have mentioned above. In this emergence of what are termed 'poor' Churches—something which we encounter in rather abstract terms with such concepts as the grassroots Church, theologies of liberation, etc.—we find the attempt to invoke the grace of God as man's total liberation and the readiness to pay the price for this historical conjugation of grace and freedom. Here a start is made on overcoming the reduction of theology, whether in its privatistic or in its rationalistic version: what is involved is a new unity of the experience of redemption and of liberation, a Church community which, united with its bishops and thus incorporated in the apostolic succession, is struggling for a new relationship (and one which admittedly is not free from conflict) between religion and society, between mysticism and politics.

For us in our overcomplex situation in the late Western world this may often seem too much of an oversimplification, too pre-theological, as it were, too much of a hermeneutical distortion, too uncritical. But when we look more closely we see that this hermeneutic of the awareness of danger, in which the business of faith and of theology is taken seriously, as a result forces together in a new way things that with us are abstractly separated and split up: theory and practice, logic and mysticism, grace and suffering, spirit and resistance. Here we see a 'reduction' that is quite other than a wicked and deceitful emasculation of the relations of theology and faith. Its stimulus must have a retroactive effect, in a thoroughly reformist manner, on the late Western situation of the Church and theology, so that in our situation we may survive the damage, the thoroughly traumatic injuries inflicted by the modern age.[7] This is of course not the complete answer to the question about the fate of theology with regard to the modern age, but it is, I hope, a prospect.

Translated by Robert Nowell

Notes

1. On this, see F. Fiorenza 'Religion and Politik' in *Christlicher Glaube in moderner Gesellschaft*, Teilband 27 (Freiburg) 1982. For a topical controversy in this context see J. Moltmann 'Das Gespenst einer Zivilreligion', in *Evangelische Kommentare* (March) 1983.

2. On this, see J. B. Metz *Jenseits bürgerlicher Religion* (1980).

3. See *Mythos und Moderne*, ed. K. H. Bohrer (Frankfurt 1983).

4. For the social constitution of theological reason, see W. Kroh *Kirche im gesellschaftlichen Widerspruch* (Munich 1982).

5. Where I go along with Karl Rahner: see *Schriften zur Theologie*, vol. XIV pp. 287ff.

6. For example in those of a Lévi-Strauss.

7. On this mutual creativity and assimilation, see J. B. Metz *Jenseits bürgerlicher Religion* (1980) and M. Lamb *Solidarity with Victims* (New York 1982).

Virgil Elizondo

Conditions and Criteria for Authentic Inter-Cultural Theological Dialogue

INTRODUCTION

ON THE morning of Pentecost, peoples 'from all the nations' in the world were gathered together. When they heard the Galileans speak they were astonished because each one heard them 'in his native tongue' (Acts 2:8). The Pentecost narrative is both symbolic of what the new assembly of believers will be and normative for all the efforts of Christians to bring about world unity. The unity of Pentecost does not destroy the different languages and cultures. Rather it affirms them in their identity while opening them up to otherness through the principle of universal love which is now operative in them. This universal love does not destroy the local identity, but it does destroy the natural ghettoisation of all human groups. Already in the first century, after a short and painful struggle at efforts of uniformity, the small group of insignificant believers dared to think of themselves as universal, not because they included all peoples but precisely because through the principle of universal love they were now disposed to break through all socio-cultural barriers of separation so as to accept all peoples into their ranks as equal—masters or slaves, Jews or Gentiles, men or women, important or insignificant.

It should not be surprising to discover the great diversity of churches which immediately blossomed in the first century of the Christian movement and the great liberty and creativity of theological reflection which characterised the early churches as seen in Fathers of the Church. The new movement struggled to cross the various frontiers which kept persons and peoples apart so as to bring about the new unity of the human family. Yet in so doing, it did not seek to destroy the peoples but to bring them into a new way of life within their own socio-cultural context. Thus they could become Jewish-Christians, Jewish-Hellenistic Christians and Greek Christians. The cultural identity was not destroyed but the exclusivity of the culture was indeed destroyed.

Babel is synonymous with confusion and division, while Pentecost is synonymous with oneness, understanding and unity. Quite often, in the very name of the unity of Pentecost, we perpetrate the imperialistic divisions of Babel and in the name of the forced unity of Babel, we fear and struggle against the unity of Pentecost.

'That all may be one' has been and continues to be the quest of Christians. The unity of the human family has been one of the original and persistent characteristics of the Christian movement. Yet the way in which this oneness has been perceived has certainly varied. The unity of the one universal communion in the local churches seems to be dawning with the beginning of the third millennium. Unity and universality are two important characteristics of the Church, yet the understanding of unity and universality can be as diverse as day is from night.

Since the advent of John XXIII and Vatican Council II, the quest for unity through dialogue has been going on at various levels and developing with increasing momentum, ecumenical dialogue, the inter-religious quest, and the dialogue with other humanitarian groups. All these dialogues have been characterised by a deep mutual respect of the fundamental goodness of each of the dialoguing parties and a serious effort to listen very carefully to what each one of the partners is trying to say. No one has tried to convert the others, but all have struggled together to grow in the appreciation of the goodness which exists in each one.

We now turn our attention to a new dimension of the dialogue: the *intra-ecclesial inter-cultural dialogue*. Because the entire edifice of the Church—its dogmas, laws, moral codes, theologies and rituals—has been increasingly shaped by the centuries of Western symbolic systems and Western intellectual patterns of thought, this new dialogue will be much more difficult and equally much more fascinating. An authentic intercultural dialogue within the Church will touch on aspects of Church life which have heretofore remained untouched and sacrosanct. Furthermore questions will be asked not from the perspective of the relationship of the Church to others, but in the name of the very unity and catholicity of the Church. Differences will emerge which at first will appear to divide the Church but which in effect will have the potential of bringing about a much more authentic unity.

For the Church to be a living and visible sacrament of the unity of Pentecost *three conditions* will be necessary.

1. ECCLESIAL CONDITIONS

The fundamental condition for the possibility of an authentic intercultural theological dialogue is the heartfelt acceptance of the authenticity of the local church. This is more easily accepted in the young churches[1] of the world which were born as a result of the missionary efforts of the past four centuries. However, it seems to be quite difficult to accept by the old churches[2] of the North Atlantic countries which still tend to look upon themselves as 'the Church' while considering the other churches of the world as merely local. Even when the authenticity of the local church is accepted, it will not be easy to work out the implications.

(a) On the part of the young churches

It will be necessary for them to discover their own way in accordance with the guidance of *Ad Gentes*:

> From the customs and traditions of their people, from their wisdom and their learning, from their arts and sciences, these churches borrow all those things which can contribute to the glory of their Creator, the revelation of the Saviour's grace, or the proper arrangement of Christian life.

> If this goal is to be achieved, theological investigation must necessarily be stirred up in each major socio-cultural area, as it is called. In this way under the light of the tradition of the universal Church, a fresh scrutiny will be brought to bear on the deeds and words which God has made known . . .

> Thus it will be more clearly seen in what ways faith can seek for understanding in the philosophy and wisdom of these peoples . . .[3]

Because the weight of the interiorised 'Christian' culture of the West is so strong, it will frequently be difficult for the young churches to distinguish between the core of the Christian message and its socio-cultural formulation and expression. As stated by John XXIII at the opening sessions of the Second Vatican Council: 'The substance of the ancient doctrine of the deposit of faith is one thing and the way in which it is presented is another.'

Through the proclamation of the Gospel, new churches are implanted which are endowed with their own vitality and socio-cultural characteristics. As these develop, it is not a question of merely translating or adapting the theologies of the North Atlantic into the native languages, but of allowing the new community of believers to grow and develop in the Christian faith alive in them.

In this new reality, reminiscent of the patristic times[4] no one will think of doing theology in isolation from the believing community. The theological questions will emerge out of the common needs, struggles, questions and tensions of the community. The fundamental books to be consulted will be the life-tensions of the community. The language to be used will be that of the people as conditioned by their own historical-cultural identity. The theologian becomes the person of analysis, dialogue, and creative (prophetic) proclamation. Analysis will help the community to probe and clarify the actual reality of their living faith; dialogue will assist the local group to understand and appreciate its own situation in the light of the tradition of the Church, especially the foundational traditions of the New Testament; and creative proclamation will help to formulate the new faith-alternatives of the present moment. The creative proclamation will be prophetic because it will unveil the hidden evil of the local situation and announce new challenges and possibilities which had previously been unsuspected. It is in the context of the real situation of the life of the faith community that the sacramental and doctrinal life of the Church must be consistently re-thought and reformulated so that the core may continue to be maintained while its outward expressions and local implications can change with the changing circumstances.

It is important that the theologians of the young churches do not feel that they have to imitate the cultural patterns of Europe. Some exciting break-throughs are already beginning to take place in Latin America, Africa, India and Japan. They are just beginning. The new theologians should not feel that they have to 'prove' themselves to their 'European Masters' but rather they should be concerned that they are truly exercising their ministry of theologising with and for their own local church. It is there that the validity of their work has to be verified.

The temptations of the theologians of the young churches will be to try to imitate the manner, vocabulary and method of the old parent churches. In their very struggles to emerge with a theological reflection which is faithful to their own native culture, they will often be held back by their own constant reference to the theological philosophical works of the old churches. While the ways of the old should not be rejected automatically simply because they are old or European, neither should they become the necessary points of reference or normative models for all theologians. These approaches may or may not be valid for the old churches, that is for them to discover, but they are not necessarily true or valid approaches for the new churches. Theologians like Amalorpavadas of India, Pieris of Sri Lanka, and Gutierrez and Boff of Latin America, are certainly examples of the theologians of the new churches.

At this moment of history it is the mission of the young churches to come forth with new creativity which will enrich not only their own local churches but the entire *communio* of churches. They should not waste their time seeking to be legitimised by the theologians of the old Church, but should strive to produce something truly new which is both in fidelity to the core of the Christian message and in fidelity to the 'genius and disposition of each culture' (AG 22). Only from this position, will they be prepared to enter into an authentic fraternal dialogue with the other churches of the world.

(b) On the part of the old churches

I suspect that their own personal acceptance of the reality of their own church as local will be much more difficult. They are encumbered by centuries of tradition of seeing themselves as THE Church and their missionaries carried their model of Church to many parts of the world as if it were the one and only model of the Church. This myopia was simply the product of the interiorised culture of the Church seeing itself through the optic of the empire or the optic of the sociological model of the monarchy.

It will not be easy for the old churches to recognise that what the young churches are called upon to do they too must do for their own people. In this respect, the 'mother churches' (the original missionary-sending churches which gave birth to new churches) will now have to begin learning from their children churches who have now come of age and have joined the *communio* of churches as equal partners. As long as the old churches do not come to this recognition in realistic and practical terms, they will continue to think of themselves as 'universal' while seeing the new churches of the Third World as 'local'.

Even though the task of theology has often been restricted to the university in the North Atlantic community, the freshness of the theologising of the Third World can be directional to the old churches: theology can be returned to its legitimate place as a pastoral service in the midst of the believing community. The theologians of the Third World have had no choice. Because of the poverty of their situation, they have been providentially forced to remain in close contact and in solidarity with the questions and struggles of their people. However, for the theologians of the old churches culturally conditioned by centuries of academic theology, it will not be easy to recapture the theologising styles of the early Fathers of the Church which are re-flourishing today in the peripheral areas of Christianity.[5]

(c) On the part of the Church of Rome

There is no question that Rome, in its official statements, encourages the development of local churches with their theologies. As Rahner has stated: 'Even according to explicit declarations the Apostolic See is convinced that the future unity of the Church will not mean reducing all the (Christian) churches to a uniformity modeled on the present-day Roman Church of the West, but that the particular churches in uniting with Peter may and should retain to the greatest possible extent their own laws, their fidelity to their own tradition and history. . . .'[6]

Yet it is equally evident that when this really begins to happen, there are fears, difficulties and warnings. The specific developments which take place as the new local churches grow and mature are not easy for a central government which has been accustomed to centuries of absolute control and regulation. The same spirit of openness and respect which is evident in dialogue with others outside the Catholic communion is not always accorded to dialogue within the same household. New aspects of theological expressions, church life and liturgical celebrations will emerge whose concrete and practical consequences will not be easily appreciated by Rome any more than initially Peter was able to appreciate the practical consequences of the authentic catholicity of the faith which he himself professed (Gal. 2). In a true exchange of teaching and learning the true catholicity of the Church will continue to grow, deepen and extend while avoiding the dangers of ecclesial nationalism. In such a fellowship, the role of Rome as the servant of unity will not diminish, but its function and image will certainly be different.

In summary, there are three ecclesial conditions that are fundamental pre-requisites

c

for an authentic intercultural theological dialogue: (i) For the young churches to be firmly secured in their own identity and in their own style of theologising; (ii) for the old churches of the North Atlantic nations to discover that they too are local churches with the need to de-universalise themselves and begin to enjoy their own unique local status; (iii) for the local church of Rome to rediscover in practice what it means to be the centre of unity versus the centre of control, imposition and regulation.

2. PERSONAL CONDITIONS

There will be several personal attitudes which will be fundamental for any sincere dialogue to be possible.

(a) Personal conversion

For an intra-ecclesial dialogue to take place the first condition will be the ongoing conversion from one's own socio-cultural absolutes to the way of Jesus. It is amazing how many household gods each one of us possesses. A conversion to the way of Jesus which relativises everything which is not God is fundamental for a real dialogue among equals, otherwise, we will be more playing God than mutually seeking God's way for all. The first personal condition for dialogue is the realisation of each theologian that he/she does not have a monopoly on the truth and that only in Jesus will we gradually come to the fullness of truth—a fullness which is more eschatological than temporal.

Through our conversion we will enter into a world of radical love for others, especially the poor, the marginated, the exploited, and the public sinners of the world. Poverty and suffering, being universal, transcend Church, doctrine and theology and can become the basis of authentic dialogue, challenging everyone to the common Christian struggle. Because we love, we will be driven to see new aspects of people and of nations that we have not previously suspected.

This love for others will lead us beyond our ordinary 'self-centred' existence to an 'other-centred' existence which will create within us a desire to know more profoundly about the other. It is this other-centred existence which will impel us to seek to understand others not from our own criteria of judgment but as they truly are and as they themselves see themselves. It is amazing how in these very efforts to know the other as the other is will we begin to discover aspects of ourselves and our own people which we had not understood before. The more we are secure in our historical-cultural identity, the less threatened we will be by otherness. To know and accept ourselves as we are, without trying to prove ourselves to anyone is the beginning of the necessary openness-otherness. Often it is the ones who do not know themselves who are very threatened by otherness and thus become very defensive about their own cultural identity and way of life.

(b) Humility

Another fundamental condition for inter-cultural theological dialogue will be a profound sense of our own humility: 'Never act out of rivalry or conceit. Rather let all parties think humbly of others as superior to themselves, each of you looking to others' interests rather than his own' (Phil. 2:3). This humility is most important. It does not mean putting ourselves down as if we were worthless. We are simply one of the fellowship. This biblical humility means that we accept ourselves as we are—historically and culturally conditioned. This is both our originality and our limitation. As original, we have much to offer; as limited, we have much to learn. It is in this same spirit that we accept all others—neither as superior or inferior, masters or students. It is this humility which gives us the spontaneous willingness to offer what we have without apologies and to receive from others without a sense of shame. We are different, but united in the common enterprise of the Kingdom.

In this humility, we do not demand of others that they meet our standards or expectations in order to dialogue. Rather, we seek to understand them as they are. We do not seek to judge or evaluate, but to understand and appreciate. It is true that this intense listening to others will challenge us to see ourselves in ways which we have not suspected but this is the very redeeming and liberating nature of authentic dialogue. Without threats or arguments, each of the interlocutors begins to see new aspects of the truth which were previously unseen. Thus dialogue is not simply the good feeling of being together. It involves the risk of being challenged, the vulnerability of being known in one's own weakness, and the possibility of discovering that one might be wrong. Yet, dialogue is not an argument; it is not, *per se*, a confrontation, but the common struggle of arriving at truth.

(c) Patient hope

As the world becomes smaller, a global village as it were, the various cultural-linguistic regions of the world become more and more aware of the various approaches to truth. The West appears to give a priority to the rational, the East to contemplation, the North to pragmatic thought, the South to imagery, religious symbolism and political action. These are not contradictory but complementary to the integral human condition. In today's world strongly conditioned by the great Western expansion of the last four centuries, questions of economic, technological, cultural and religious domination cannot be ignored. The interiorised models of the North Atlantic nations cannot be overlooked. The needed humility for an authentic dialogue will necessitate a strong liberation experience on the part of all the partners.

Because of the very nature of the complexity of the various cultural regions of the world, further complicated by the economic divisions between the rich and the poor nations of the world, and between the poor and the rich within each nation, the dialogue will be slow and often painful. Hope and patience will be necessary for all who embark on this exciting venture. It is never easy to relativise our values and systems of thought. They are so deeply engrained within us that we presuppose they are the same for every other normal human being. It takes a real dying to self to realise that there can be other legitimate values and systems of thought. Only through patient listening which is willing to put aside the prejudgments which stem from our inculturated values will we be able to truly enter the world of the other.

The patient struggle will be animated by the hope that gradually we can arrive at a composite consensus of our understanding and expression of faith. I say a composite consensus because the truth of God and of the human person cannot be exhausted by the thought patterns and expressions of any one people, culture or nation. Yet each one will have something to contribute which can enrich the others—like the various colours of a beautiful painting. It is through this patient dialogue that each participant will at one and the same time come into a deeper awareness of their own cultural identity and partici-pate more and more in the world of others. No one will cease being who they are but each will become much more of a human being, for to enter into the world of others does not destroy the self but only the selfishness.

3. STRUCTURES FOR DIALOGUE

Besides the ecclesiology of the local church and the personal attitudes that are prerequisites for dialogue, structures have to develop that will allow this dialogue to take place at the level of the community of the churches and not at the interpersonal level of individual theologians. In some ways this has already taken place. Vatican II and the subsequent Synods of Bishops provided opportunities for the beginnings of intercultural theological dialolgue. The Asiatic, African and Latin American and Episcopal meetings also provided for this in a limited way. *Concilium* itself is providing a forum for theologians from the various regions of the world to share their thought with their colleagues throughout the world—both to teach and to be enriched. The Ecumenical Third World Theologians Association has provided for the beginnings of such dialogue amongst the theologians of the Third World. The encounters have been most enriching. The general assemblies and chapters of international religious groups are also providing for such opportunities.

For authentic intercultural dialogue to really take place, however, a whole attitude of theological reflection must begin at a very grassroots level of each diocesan church. The Gospel must be in constant dialogue with each believing community deeply rooted in its own history and society. Only through this patient dialogue will the authentic theological thought of each local believing community come forth. From this grassroots movement, opportunities for diocesan, regional, national and international dialogue have to be provided. Such opportunities will come through centres or institutes of theological research both at the regional and international level. Encounters amongst theologians who are already engaged in this type of theological reflection will also prove most helpful.

The goals of an authentic intercultural theological dialogue are not to reduce anyone's opinion to that of someone else but to allow the entire Catholic Church to grow in unity and universality. The unity of the gradually developing consensus which will be made up of the many aspects of the one truth which will be explored and presented by the various churches. In universality because while no one will be destroyed everyone will be enriched in this process of dialogue. It will be through the ongoing love of one another and quest for authentic Christian unity that we will all come into a deeper appreciation and awareness of our Catholicity.

Notes

1. By 'young churches' I mean the churches of the Third World which were born out of the evangelising/colonising movements of the last four centuries.
2. By 'old churches' I refer to the churches of Europe. I also include the churches of the USA and Canada since they were not born out of missionary efforts but were simply the continuation of the European churches carried over by the immigrants.
3. *Ad Gentes* of Vatican II, no. 22.
4. C. Kannengiesser, 'Avenir des traditons fondatrices' in *Recherches de science religieuse* 65 (1977).
5. *Ibid.*
6. As quoted by M. Azevedo *Inculturation and the Challenges of Modernity* (Rome 1982) p. 55.

PART II

The Word for the Whole Church of Particular Theologies

Gustavo Gutiérrez

Speaking about God

REFLECTION ON the word of God is linked to the way this is experienced and proclaimed within the Christian community. When a theology becomes deeply and courageously involved in the situation in which the Church finds itself at any given moment of its history, then it will continue to be meaningful even once the context in which it arose has passed. Permanence in essentials results from theology's ability to take root in the real problems of its time and in the experience of the faith of a particular body of followers of Christ. This is undoubtedly why the works of Augustine of Hippo and Thomas Aquinas, to take only two great names from the past, can still speak to us so challengingly today.

Over the last two centuries the theology elaborated in the classical centres of study has had to take account of the state of affairs resulting from what has come to be known as modern mentality. This has emerged over a long period, but received a decisive push forward from the industrial and social revolutions of the eighteenth century, as from the intellectual understanding of these processes which we call the Enlightenment. The Church then found itself living in a social and intellectual milieu deeply critical of the faith and of the Christian life style. This time is still with us. While some of its aspects have been superseded by time, others have been heightened. So theological reflection still has to tackle its task in such a way as to give new vitality to the proclamation of the word of God in the modern world.

But at the same time, a new situation, brought about by the modern era itself, has begun to emerge. This consists of the increasingly energetic and extensive presence of the poor and oppressed on the stage of world history. This has often come about suddenly and in unforeseen ways. So new conditions of life for the Christian community have been created. Society and the Church today have, so to speak, been invaded by the poor. But if one looks at the process more closely, its suddenness will be seen to be more apparent than real. Its historical roots in fact go deep; this, in turn, ensures the persistence of this historical event and shows that it cannot be regarded as a passing phenomenon.

The theological schools that are growing up in the so-called Third World countries, or among the racially and culturally oppressed minorities of the wealthy nations, or in the context of women's liberation, are expressions of the new presence of those who have previously been 'absent' from history. Their efforts spring from areas of humanity that have previously been arid, theologically speaking, but in which Christian faith has old and deep roots. Hence their present fruitfulness.

One expression, among others, of this new presence is the reflection on faith in the context of Latin America that has come to be known as liberation theology, and I propose to take its approach as the basis for this article. Two great quests and an overriding concern have been, and still are, central to this approach. These are, on one hand, the question of method in theology and the adoption of the point of view of the poor in theological thinking; on the other, the need to proclaim the Gospel for the Christian community in our midst. These are the points I want to deal with here. They were the first concerns of liberation theology, historically speaking, but they also remain *basic* to it in the sense that they have kept their relevance and their capacity for assimilation to new contributions.

1. FINDING A WAY

(a) All theology is speaking about God. In the final analysis this is its only subject. The God of Jesus Christ is presented as a mystery. So any sensible theology will realise that it is trying something very difficult, if not impossible, in thinking and speaking about this mystery. Hence Thomas Aquinas' famous phrase: 'What we do not know about God is greater than what we do know'. We need to be clear on this point when starting out on any discourse about faith. This is what the Peruvian writer Jose María Arguedas means by saying—outside a strictly theological context—'What we know is far less than the great hope we feel'. God, in fact, is rather the object of hope—which respects his mystery—than of knowledge.

So how do we find a way of speaking about God? Liberation theology would say that God is first contemplated and practised, and only then thought about. What we mean by this is that worshipping God and doing his will are the necessary condition for thinking about him. Only on the basis of mysticism and practice is it possible to work out an authentic and respectful way of speaking about God. In practice, and specifically in our approach to the poor, we meet the Lord, but at the same time this meeting makes our solidarity with the poor deeper and more meaningful. Contemplation and involvement in history are two essential and interrelated dimensions of Christian life. The mystery is revealed in contemplation and in solidarity with the poor: this is what we call the *first act or step*, Christian life; only after this can this life inspire a process of reasoning: this is the *second act or step*.

Contemplating and putting into practice both form, in a certain way, the time for *silence* before God. Keeping silent is the condition for loving encounter-prayer with God and commitment to God. Experiencing the inadequacy of words to express what we live at the deepest level will make our language both richer and more modest. Theology is a way of speaking enriched by silence. This can be shown schematically thus:[1]

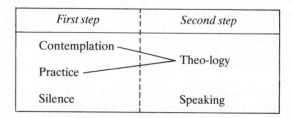

First step	*Second step*
Contemplation	Theo-logy
Practice	
Silence	Speaking

(b) The distinction between these two steps is a key point in theological method, that is in the procedure (method, from *hodos*, way) to be followed if we are to think in the light of faith. This point is certainly far more traditional than many people think, but what I want to stress here is that this approach is not limited just to theological methodology but implies a way of living, a way of being and making oneself a disciple of Jesus Christ.

In the book that relates the *Acts* of the first Christian community, the community is called something special and original: the Way. The term is generally used on its own, without qualifications. Following the *way* implies certain *conduct*: the Greek word *hodos* in fact means both things. Christians are distinguished by a behaviour, a life style. This is what sets the Christian community apart from the Jewish and pagan worlds in which it lived and gave its witness. This conduct was a way of thinking and of acting, 'as the Spirit dictates' (Rom. 8:4).

The way *to be* Christian is the basis of the route to follow in order *to do* theology. Our methodology is our spirituality (that is, a way of being Christian). Reflection on the mystery of God can only be done from following Jesus. Only by walking according to the Spirit is it possible to think about and proclaim the gratuitous love of the Father for each and every human person. It is perhaps this relationship between the Christian life and theological method that has made the Latin American base communities become the agents of this theological approach.

All Christian life begins with conversion. This implies breaking with personal and social sin and taking a new course. This is the necessary condition for welcoming the coming Kingdom (see Mark 1:14). Conversion means stepping aside from our own way (see Luke 10:29-37) and walking in the path of the other, our neighbour, the poor in particular. This is also the condition for a fruitful theological understanding. Going into the world of the poor is a long and at times painful process, but there we meet the One about whom theology is called to speak. Besides being difficult, this process is often risky, so this speaking is often speaking about the God of life.

2. . . . FROM THE POOR

(*a*) Latin American society is characterised by the poverty that Puebla called 'inhuman' (n. 29) and 'anti-evangelical' (n. 1159). In the famous phrase of Medellín, it constitutes a situation of 'institutionalised violence' (Peace, 16).

Today we can see ever more clearly what this situation implies: quite simply, poverty means death. Death through hunger or sickness, or from the repressive methods of those who see their privileges endangered by every attempt to liberate the oppressed. To this physical death can be added a cultural death, since the dominator seeks to annihilate all that gives unity and strength to the dispossessed of this world so as to make them fall an easy prey to the machinery of oppression. This is the setting for the social analysis that forms part of our theological endeavour, helping us to understand what particular forms this reality of death takes in Latin America.

This is what we mean when we speak of poverty, of the destruction of people and peoples, of cultures and traditions. In particular the poverty of the most despoiled groups: Indians, Blacks, and their women who are doubly marginalised and oppressed. So we are not, as is sometimes thought, simply faced with a 'social situation', something that might be considered alien to the basic requirements of the Gospel message. No, what we have here is something contrary to the Kingdom of life proclaimed by the Lord.

(*b*) Experiencing the unjust death of so many people in Latin America helps us understand better the injustice of Jesus' death. And in its turn the 'scandal of the Cross' sheds light on our situation and sharpens the contrast between this situation and the gift of life in Christ.

In the dramatic account of Jesus' trial given in the Gospel of John, we see him move from accused to judge. The leaders of his people go so far as to betray their own nationalist convictions ('we have no king except Caesar'). The Cross, in Johannine theology, becomes the throne of this 'Man' identified with the poor of this world (Matt. 25:31-46) who is at the same time king. King of a kingdom of life revealed precisely in his death on the Cross, or more exactly in his victory over this death, in the Resurrection.

We should judge the premature and unjust deaths of the great majority of the inhabitants of our sub-continent in the light of this life that passes through death. Such a judgment will show us that what we call 'internal liberation'—a classic theme in the theology of liberation—means in the final analysis acceptance of the gift of the kingdom of life. Life involving all human dimensions, according to God's overall will, and therefore contrary to the situation of the unjust death of the poor and oppressed. A state of affairs which is therefore called, from a theological point of view, a 'situation of sin' by both Medellín and Puebla.

(c) For this reason, because the gift of life must lead us to reject unjust death, the ultimate motive for solidarity with the poor resides in the God in whom we believe. There can be, and there are, other valid motives: the sufferings of the people today, a social analysis of the situation—essential if we are to understand the historical causes of this state of affairs—, recognition of the poor as protagonists of their own history. But ultimately, for the Christian, his commitment is theocentrically based; it is based in our faith in God, the God of life revealed in Jesus Christ. This commitment is linked to the centre of our faith in God and hope for the coming of the Kingdom. The Lord is at the centre of our lives, and the rest is extra.

3. . . . TO BEAR WITNESS TO THE RESURRECTION

To make disciples of all nations (see Matt. 28:19) was the task enjoined by the Risen Lord on his disciples in Galilee, the very place where Jesus had preached. The universality of the message is thus marked with the particularity of this forgotten and despised land of Galilee.[2]

(a) It is not easy to root our speaking about God in the world of poverty and oppression. It combines deep joys and an enormous creative capacity with great sufferings and the permanent threat of frustration and despair. So in Latin America even those who try to struggle against the ruling injustice face threats from different sources. The situation in which we live is plagued with both difficulties and possibilities, with equivocal proposals and despairing solutions, but also with paths that respect the deepest human values; with the upsurge of incredible egoisms and pretensions of all kinds, but also with humble and limitless generosities; with desires to overthrow everything, but also with creative initiatives that respect the most valuable traditions of the Latin American people.

This seething world questions our way of being Christians and demands both political and spiritual discernment. We need to listen to its questioning if we wish to listen to what the Lord has to tell us through our own history.

(b) The challenge posed to theological thought in Latin America is how to find a way of speaking about God that springs from the situation created by the unjust poverty in which the great majority of the people—the despised races, the exploited social classes, the alienated cultures, the women discriminated against, live. At the same time our language has to be one fed by the hope which buoys up a people struggling for its liberation. Our understanding of our faith has to be continually rooted in this mixture of sufferings and joys, of uncertainties and certainties, of generosity and deceit.

I think it can be said that both a prophetic and a mystical way of speaking about God are coming to birth in these lands of horror and hope. The language of contemplation recognises that everything comes from the gratuitous love of the Father. The language of prophecy denounces the situation—and its structural causes—of injustice and robbery in which the poor of Latin America live. This is what Puebla means when it talks of 'recognising the suffering features of Christ the Lord' in all those faces marked by the sufferings of an oppressed people (31).

Without prophecy, the language of contemplation runs the risk of failing to bite on the history in which God acts and in which we meet him. And without the mystical dimension, prophetic language can narrow its horizons and weaken its perception of the One who makes all things new. 'Sing to the Lord, praise the Lord, for he has delivered the needy from the power of evil men' (Jer. 20:13). Singing and deliverance, thanksgiving and demand for justice. This is the challenge facing a Christian life that seeks to be faithful to the God of Jesus Christ beyond possible spiritual evasions and political reductionisms.

(c) These two ways of speaking about God seek to communicate the gift of the kingdom of God revealed in the life, death and Resurrection of Jesus. This is the nucleus of the message, which we are rediscovering through our situation, and which calls us as a community, as an *ecclesia*, and within which we try to think about our faith. Theology is an ecclesial function. It is done in a Church which should bear witness in history to a life that overcomes death. Bearing witness to the Resurrection means opting for life. For all expressions of life, since nothing escapes the all-embracingness of the Kingdom of God. This witness to life (material and spiritual life, personal and social life, present and future life) takes on special importance in an area marked by early and unjust death, but also by efforts at freeing itself from oppression. The situation of death and sin is a negation of the resurrection. So the witness to the resurrection will be the one who can ask with the same irony as St Paul, 'Death where is your victory?'—the question prompted by a witness such as that of Mgr. Romero, for example.

This is the life we celebrate in the Eucharist, the prime task of the ecclesial community. In the breaking of bread we bring to mind the love and faithfulness of Jesus which brought him to his death, and the confirmation of his mission to the poor through the resurrection. The breaking of the bread is at once the starting point and the destination of the Christian community. In it we express deep communion in human suffering—so often brought on by lack of bread—and recognise, in joy, the Risen Lord who gives life and raises the hopes of the people brought together by his actions and his word.

Liberation theology seeks to be a way of speaking about God. It is an attempt to make the word of life present in a world of oppression, of injustice, of death.

Translation by Paul Burns

Notes

1. The creative capacity shown by a poor, believing people, its spontaneous generosity, its facility for creating symbols and for demonstrating its feelings, are undoubtedly potential in everyone, but are often held back and repressed by certain cultural moulds. But it so happens that for the poor they are usually their only means of self-expression. An example would be the religious music of black slave cultures in North America and other places. The different Indian cultures of Latin America can also show fine examples of this capacity.

2. This is something of which Mexican-American theology has forcefully reminded us recently.

Elisabeth Schüssler Fiorenza

For Women in Men's Worlds:
A Critical Feminist Theology of Liberation

> This is a poem for me
> and women like me
> we who live in men's worlds
> like the free spirits of birds in the sky . . .[1]

FEMINIST WRITERS and poets explore the experiences of women in androcentric culture and patriarchal society. They seek for a new voice, a 'common language' that could express the meaning and significance of women's lives and could articulate the religious experience of 'trying to be in our souls'.[2] In 1896 Alice Meynell who was one of the greatest English poets of her time but is virtually forgotten today—likened such a woman thinker to the biblical figure of the Good Shepherd: 'She walks—the lady of my delight—a shepherdess of sheep.' She guards the flock of her thoughts 'so circumspect and right: She has her soul to keep.'[3] In a similar vein the black poet Ntozake Shange ends her choreopoem *'for colored girls who have considered suicide/when the rainbow is enuf'* with an affirmation born out of the exploration of black women's pain and oppression: 'i found god in myself . . . & i loved her fiercely.'[4]

Just as feminist poets so also feminist theologians seek to articulate what it means that women have found God in our soul—soul not understood as over and against body and world but as religious and spiritual self, as the feminist vision of self-affirmation and freedom lived in men's worlds and expressed in the oppressor's language. Within the patriarchal context of Christian religion women's spirit has continued to explode from time to time proclaiming truth and justice. However for the most part such articulations of women's spiritual experiences were swallowed up by historical forgetfulness and covered up by androcentric language.

For the first time in Christian history we women no longer seek to express our experience of God's Spirit within the frameworks of androcentric spirituality but attempt to articulate that we have found God in our soul in such a way that this experience of her presence can transform and break through the traditional frameworks of androcentric theology and patriarchal church. For the first time in Christian history women have achieved sufficient theological education and economic-institutional independence to refuse to be just the objects of men's theologising and to become the initiating subjects of theology and spirituality.

We Christian women have begun to formulate our own theological questions, to explore our own Christian history, and to chart our own spiritual visions. The theology which we have learnt, has left us out, the history of the Church is not written as women's history, and the clerical-patriarchal structures of Church identify it as a men's church.[5] In her article 'In the Shadow of the Father' Hildegunde Wöller has articulated this alienating experience of women studying theology: 'Theology and life remained unmediated in myself. A dream plagued me several years: again and again the same dream: I came home and found in my bed a child about whose existence I had known nothing and whom I had forgotten. It was starved and frozen to death. Nobody had heard it crying. I felt innocent.'[6] Only when she attempted the journey inward to take care of the lost child did she realise that the Gospel addressed her self. But when she began to communicate this experience those whom she had called her 'theological fathers' did not understand her and labelled her religious experience of self 'dangerous, subjective, or irrelevant'.

FEMINIST THEOLOGY

Feminist theology is often misunderstood as a genitive theology, as the theology *of Woman*. It is misconstrued as 'feminine' theology, a theology that perpetuates the cultural-religious stereotypes of femininity and masculinity. Establishment theologians usually qualify feminist theology as 'so-called', as a somewhat dubious and academically suspect enterprise. Such prevalent and often deliberate misrepresentations of feminist theology are, of course, not accidental. By qualifying feminist theology as 'Woman's' or as 'feminine' theology it can be restricted to women who are marginalised, trivialised and considered of no importance in a patriarchal church and society. While the 'pro-feminine' expressions in theology are lauded, the characterisation 'feminist' is labelled 'radical, abrasive, fanatic, and unwomanly'. Naturally such a misrepresentation of feminist theology invites its rejection as a 'particularistic' theology restricted to a tiny minority in society and church—militant women—with whom no 'real' woman should want to be associated.

The early feminists assumed that the intellectual frameworks as well as the contents of academic education and scientific knowledge available to men but not to women were valid, true, humanistic, and objective. If women just could overcome their exclusion from academic institutions and the professions they could fully participate in the production of human knowledge and art. One of the first to question this assumption was Virginia Woolf who insisted in *Three Guineas* that women must raise the question whether they should join the 'processions of educated men'.[7] They had to decide under what terms and conditions women should join them and to inquire where the processions of the sons of educated men would lead them. The feminist studies movement within the second wave of the women's movement has explicitly addressed these questions.

The resurgence of the women's liberation movement has not just revived women's political struggles for equal rights and full access to academic institutions but also inaugurated an intellectual revolution that engenders a paradigm shift[8] from an androcentric world-view and intellectual framework to a feminist comprehension of the world, human history, and Christian religion. While androcentric scholarship takes *man* (male) as the paradigmatic human being feminist scholarship[9] insists on the reconceptualisation of our intellectual frameworks in such a way that they become truly inclusive of women as subjects of human scholarship and knowledge on the one hand and articulate male experience and insights as a particular experience and perception of reality and truth on the other hand.

Thus feminist scholarship throws into question the dominant cultural mind-set articulated in male language, classical male texts, scholarly frameworks and theories of men that make invisible, marginalise and trivialise women. Such an androcentric world view perpetuates a popular and scientific consciousness that declares women's experiences, cultural contributions, scientific knowledge, and artistic or religious expressions as less valuable, less significant, or less worthy than those of men. Feminist studies challenge male symbolic representations, historical interpretations, and our habitual consciousness of sexism as a classificatory given in our language and thought-world. They point to the interaction between language and society, sexual stereotypes and economic exploitation, gender and race as social constructs and political oppression, to the interface of sexism, colonialism, and militarism in Western society. Sexism, racism, colonialism, and militarism are thereby unmasked as constitutive of the language of oppression in our society,[10] a language that is declared as value-neutral and objective in academic discourse.

However, it must be noted that Feminist Studies articulate the feminist paradigms in different ways and with the help of varying philosophical or sociological-political analyses.[11] While e.g. liberal feminism insists on the autonomy and equal rights of the individual, socialist or Marxist feminists see the relationship between social class and gender within Western capitalism as determinative of women's societal oppression. Third World feminists in turn insist that the interactions of racism, colonialism, and sexism are defining women's oppression and struggle for liberation.[12] Such a variety of analyses and theoretical perspectives results in different conceptions of feminism, women's liberation, and of being human in the world.

Such a diversity in approach and polyphony in feminist intellectual articulations is also found in feminist theology and in feminist studies in religion.[13] It is therefore misleading to speak of feminist theology as such or of *the* feminist theology without recognising many different articulations and analyses of feminist theologies.[14] These articulations do not only share in the diverse presuppositions and theoretical analyses of women's experiences but also work within diverse theological frameworks e.g., neo-orthodoxy, liberal theology, process theology, evangelical theology, or liberation theology. As theological articulations they are rooted in diverse ecclesial visions and political-religious contexts. I have defined my own theological perspective as a critical feminist theology of liberation which is indebted to historical-critical, critical-political, and liberation-theological analyses and is rooted in my experience and engagement as a Catholic Christian woman.[15]

A CRITICAL FEMINIST THEOLOGY OF LIBERATION

Such a feminist theology conceives of feminism not just as a theoretical world-view and analysis but as a women's liberation movement for societal and ecclesial change. Patriarchy is not just a 'dualistic ideology' or androcentric world-construction in language, not just the domination of all men over all women, but a social-cultural-political system of graded subjugations and dominations. Sexism, racism, and militaristic colonialism are the roots and pillars of patriarchy. Although this patriarchal system has undergone significant changes throughout its history it survives as 'capitalist patriarchy'[16] in modern societies. It has found its classic Western definition in Aristotelian philosophy which has decisively influenced not only Western political philosophy and legal systems but also Christian theology.[17]

Patriarchy defines not just women as 'the other' but it also defines subjugated peoples and races as 'the other' to be exploited and dominated in the service of powerful men. It defines women not just as 'the other' of men but also as subordinated and subjected to propertied men. It conceives of women's and coloured peoples' 'nature' in terms of their 'function' for patriarchal society which, like the patriarchal household of antiquity, is sustained by female and slave labour. Women of colour or poor women are doubly and triply oppressed in capitalist patriarchy. Patriarchy however does not just determine societal structures but also the hierarchical male structures of the Church,[18] which supports and often sustains the patriarchal structures of society that specify women's oppression not just in terms of race and class but also in terms of heterosexuality and motherhood. The right-wing backlash against the women's movement in society is legitimated and fuelled by a patriarchal Church and theology. Over and against capitalist patriarchy in society and Church, feminist theology insists that the victimisation and dehumanisation of the 'poorest and most despised woman on earth' exhibits the full death-dealing powers of patriarchal evil while poor and Third World women's struggle for survival and liberation expresses the fullest experience of God's grace and power in our midst.

Feminist theology therefore challenges all forms of liberation theology to take their preferential 'option' for the poor and oppressed seriously as the option for poor and Third World women because the majority of the poor and exploited today are women and children dependent on women for survival. As the African theologian Amba Oduyoye has pointed out: It is

> not simply a challenge to the dominant theology of the capitalist West. It is a challenge to the maleness of Christian theology worldwide, together with the patriarchal presuppositions that govern all our relationships as well as the traditional situation in which men (male human beings) reflected upon the whole of life on behalf of the whole community of women and men, young and old.[19]

In so far as feminist theology does not begin with statements about God and revelation but with the experience of women struggling for liberation from patriarchal oppression its universal character comes to the fore in the voices of women from different races, classes, cultures, and nations.[20] In so far as the primary theological question for liberation theology is not 'How can we believe in God?' but 'How can the poor achieve dignity?', the hermeneutical privilege of the poor must be articulated as the hermeneutical privilege of poor women. Liberation theology must address the patriarchal domination and sexual exploitation of women.[21] Moreover a critical feminist theology of liberation must articulate the quest for women's dignity and liberation ultimately as the quest for God.

TOWARD A WHOLE THEOLOGY

Feminist theology in the USA has insisted on the importance of 'wholeness' as a basic category in theology:[22] the integration of body and soul, world and Church, earth and heaven, immanence and transcendence, female and male, nature and human technology. Elisabeth Moltmann-Wendel has pointed out that the category of 'wholeness' did not play a role in German academic theology but is found in the religious expressions of women in the last 100 years or so.[23] A feminist theology of liberation strives for the overcoming of theological dualisms but at the same time insists that a 'whole theology' is only possible when the structures of hierarchical domination in theology and Church are overcome.

As long as women suffer the injustice and dehumanisation of societal and religious patriarchy, a feminist theology must remain first and foremost a critical theology. It must theologically name the alienation, anger, pain, and dehumanisation of women engendered by patriarchal religion. At the same time it must articulate an alternative vision of wholeness by exploring women's experiences of survival and salvation as well as by assessing Christian texts, doctrinal traditions, moral injunctions, ecclesiastical pronouncements and ecclesial structures in terms of women's liberation from patriarchal exploitation and oppression. A whole theology will only then become possible when the root of dualistic theology consisting in the contradiction between the liberating-inclusive vision of the Gospel and the cultural patriarchal structures of the hierarchical Church are overcome.

How difficult it is for women to sustain this hope of the Gospel over and against their own experience of patriarchal oppression is articulated in the following lines of a poem written by a Catholic feminist during a workshop on feminist theology:

> My mother Mary was like the original Mary in many ways.
> When she was just a little girl
>   she submitted to being raped by her father
> When she was married
>   she submitted to being beaten by my father
> When she had emotional problems
>   she submitted to shock treatment by her psychiatrist
> When she was physically ill
>   she submitted to surgery by her surgeon.
> Now she is dead—I hope God is not a father.
>
> Mary died when she was 70 in 1979.
> I held her hand and told her that she would be free
>   when she stopped breathing Our Father's air
> Her last breath was a long gasp—
>   followed by a look of peace
> The kind she had when she rocked me.
> Now she knows her heart is not a liar.
> She has escaped Our Fathers.
> Please God, let it be true.[24]

The pain and anguish that patriarchal liturgies and androcentric God-language inflict on women can only be understood when theologians and ministers realise the patriarchal dehumanisation of women in our society and Church.

Therefore a feminist theology that conceives of itself as a critical theology of liberation must sustain a creative but often painful tension. In order to remain feminist and faithful to women's experiences it must insist that Christian theology, Biblical tradition, and the Christian churches are guilty of the structural sin of sexist-racist patriarchy which perpetuates and legitimates the societal exploitation and violence against women. Patriarchal religion and theology perpetuate and legitimate rape, wife-battering, child-abuse, sexual exploitation of women, second-class citizenship and many more injustices against women. At the same time a critical feminist theology of liberation must be able to show that Christian faith, tradition and Church are *not* inherently sexist and racist, if it wants to remain a Christian theology. In order to sustain this creative tension such a feminist theology has to move critically beyond androcentric texts, traditional teachings of men, and patriarchal structures by centring on the historical struggle of self-identified women and women-identified men against sexist-racist-militarist patriarchy and for liberation in the power of the Spirit.

Such a feminist theology does not ask for the integration of women into patriarchal ecclesial structures nor does it advocate a separatist strategy but it works for the transformation of Christian symbols, tradition, and community as well as for the transformation of women. It does not derive its liberating vision from a special feminine nature nor from a metaphysical feminine principle or divinity. In exorcising the internalised sin of sexism as well as in calling the whole Christian Church to conversion feminist theology reclaims women's Christian 'birthright' of being Church, fully gifted and responsible members of the 'body of Christ' who have the power to articulate our own theology, to reclaim our own spirituality, and to determine our own and our sisters' religious life. As women-church we celebrate our vision and power for change, we ritualise our struggles, we articulate our own theological insights, and share our strength by intellectually and spiritually nurturing each other. At the same time we remain fully aware that the church of women is always the *ecclesia reformanda* in need of conversion and 'revolutionary patience' with our own failures as well as with those of our sisters.

To advocate as the 'hermeneutical centre'[25] for a feminist critical theology of liberation women's liberation struggle in society and religion, to speak of the *ekklesia* of women, does not mean to advocate a separatist strategy or to mythologise women. It means simply to make women visible as active participants and leaders in the Church, to underline women's contributions and suffering throughout Church history, and to safeguard women's autonomy and freedom from spiritual-theological patriarchal controls. Just as we speak of the church of the poor, the churches of Africa or Asia, of Presbyterian, Anglican or Roman Catholic churches without relinquishing our theological vision of the universal Catholic Christian Church, so it is also justified to speak of women-church as a manifestation of the universal Church. Since all Christian churches suffer from the structural evil of sexist-racist patriarchy in various degrees the church of women is a truly ecumenical movement that transcends traditional 'man made' denominational lines. As a feminist movement of self-identified women and women-identified men women-church defines its commitment in and through solidarity with women who suffering from the triple oppression of racism, sexism, and poverty nevertheless struggle for survival and human dignity.

I have refrained here from defining feminist theology either in terms of the traditional *topoi* of theology (God, Christ, church, sacraments, anthropology, moral theology etc.)[26] or in terms of an academic religious studies approach. Both approaches are valuable and necessary but they attempt to chart new visions and roads with the old maps of ecclesiastical or academic theology. Certainly, feminist theology could not have been born either without the women's movement for the integration of women into Church ministry and academic theology or without the pluralism and autonomy of liberal theology. Nevertheless, a critical feminist theology of liberation cannot remain within the paradigm of the 'equal rights' movement and the paradigm of liberal theology but it must call for a paradigm shift in theology and ecclesial self-understanding.

As a theology by and for women committed to the feminist liberation struggle its theoretical explorations and methodological approaches must be critically evaluated in terms of how much they are able to articulate religious visions as well as to make available theological-spiritual-institutional resources for women's liberation struggle in society and Church. Feminist theology therefore does not define itself primarily either in terms of traditional theology or ecclesial spirituality but in terms of women's struggle against societal, cultural, and religious patriarchy. As a critical theology of liberation feminist theology challenges therefore all androcentric forms of liberation theology to become more consistent and universal in their 'option for the oppressed', the majority of whom are women. At the same time, as a liberation theology it unmasks the pretence of established academic theology to be universal, objective, and value-neutral. Finally as a theology committed to the *ekklesia* of women as the gathering of free and fully responsible 'citizens' feminist theology challenges the ecclesiastical theology of seminaries and Divinity Schools to abandon its clerical particularistic self-understandings and to become a theology for the whole Church.

In short, such a feminist theology is not limited to women's interests and questions,

D

but understands itself as a different way and alternative perspective for doing theology. At the same time it insists that the androcentric-clerical theology produced in Western universities and seminaries no longer can claim to be a Catholic Christian theology if it does not become a theology inclusive of the experiences of all members of the Church, women and men, lay and clergy. Finally, it cannot claim to be a liberative theology proclaiming the 'good news' of salvation, if it does not take seriously its call to become a theology for the poor—women, men, and children—a theology subversive of all forms of sexist-racist-capitalist patriarchy. The feminist Catholic poet and social activist Renny Golden expresses this challenge to all establishment theology and churches so well:

> . . . Our freedom is your only way out.
> On the underground railroad
> you can ride with us or you become the jailer.
> Harriet Tubman never lost one entrusted to her
> Neither will we.[27]

Notes

1. From Sandra Maria Esteves 'For Tulani' in *Ordinary Women: An Anthology of Poetry by New York City Women* (New York 1978) p. 44.

2. Carol P. Christ *Diving Deep and Surfacing. Women Writers on Spiritual Quest* (Boston 1980).

3. Beverly Ann Schlack 'The "poetess of poets": Alice Meynell rediscovered' *Women's Studies* 7 (1980) pp. 111-126, 113f.

4. (New York 1976) p. 63. See also Carol Christ in the work cited in note 2, pp. 97-117.

5. See the articles in *Frauen in der Männerkirche* ed. B. Brooten/N. Greinacher (Munich-Mainz 1982).

6. Hildegunde Wöller 'Im Schatten des Vaters' in *Frau und Religion. Gotteserfahrungen im Patriarchat* ed. Elisabeth Moltmann-Wendel (Frankfurt 1983) pp. 174-177, 176 (my own translation).

7. V. Woolf *Three Guineas* (New York–London 1966) pp. 60-63.

8. See Thomas S. Kuhn *The Structure of Scientific Revolutions* (Chicago 1962); Elizabeth Janeway 'Who is Sylvia? On the Loss of Sexual Paradigms' *Signs* 5 (1980) pp. 573-589.

9. See e.g. S. Harding/M. B. Hintikka *Discovering Reality. Feminist Perspectives on Epistemology, Metaphysics, Methodology and Philosophy of Science* (Studies in Epistemology Vol 161) (Boston 1983); L. F. Pusch *Feminismus: Inspektion der Herrenkultur* (Frankfurt 1983).

10 See H. Bosmajian *The Language of Oppression* (Washington 1974); S. Trömel-Plötz *Frauensprache—Sprache der Veränderung* (Frankfurt 1982).

11. See D. Griffin Crowder 'Amazons and Mothers? Monique Wittig, Hélène Cixous and Theories of Women's Writing' *Contemporary Literature* 24/2 (1983) pp.117-144 who underlines these differences in her discussion of French and American feminism.

12. See e.g. S. A. Gonzales 'La Chicana: Guadalupe or Malinche' in *Comparative Perspective of Third World Women: The Impact of Race, Sex, and Class* ed. B. Lindsay (New York 1980) pp. 229-250.

13. See A. Barstow Driver 'Review Essay: Religion' *Signs* 2 (1976) pp. 434-442; C. P. Christ 'The New Feminist Theology: A Review of the Literature' *Religious Studies Review* 3 (1977) pp. 203-212; *Womanspirit Rising: A Feminist Reader in Religion* ed. C. P. Christ/J. Plaskow (San Francisco 1979) pp. 1-17.

14. See C. Halkes *Gott hat nicht nur starke Söhne: Grundzüge einer feministischen Theologie* (Gütersloh 1980); E. Gössmann *Die streitbaren Schwestern: Was Will die feministische Theologie?* (Freiburg 1981).

15. See my articles 'Feminist Theology as a Critical Theology of Liberation' *Theological Studies* 36 (1975) pp. 605-626; 'Towards a Liberating and Liberated Theology' *Concilium* 15 (1979) pp. 22-32; 'To Comfort or To Challenge?' *New Woman, New Church, New Priestly Ministry* ed. M. Dwyer (Rochester 1980) pp. 43-60 and my forthcoming 'Claiming the Center' in *Womanspirit Bonding*.

16. See Z. R. Eisenstein *The Radical Future of Liberal Feminism* (New York 1981) for an analysis of 'capitalist patriarchy'.

17. See my 'Discipleship and Patriarchy: Early Christian Ethos and Christian Ethics in a Feminist Perspective' in *The American Society of Christian Ethics: Selected Papers: 1982* ed. L. Rasmussen (Waterloo 1982) pp. 131-172 for a review of literature.

18. See my 'We Are Still Invisible: Theological Analysis of "Women and Ministry"' *Women and Ministry: Present Experience and Future Hopes* ed. D. Gottemoeller/R. Hofbauer (Washington 1981) pp. 29-43 and 'Emanzipation aus der Bibel' *Evangelische Kommentare* 16 (1983) pp. 195-198.

19. 'Reflections from a Third World Woman's Perspective: Women's Experience and Liberation Theologies' in *Irruption From the Third World* (New York 1983) pp. 246-255 and p. 250.

20. See especially M. Katoppo *Compassionate and Free: An Asian Woman's Theology* (New York 1980); E. Tamez *The Bible of the Oppressed* (New York 1982).

21. See especially also J. Grant 'Die schwarze Theologie und die schwarze Frau' in *Frauen in der Männerkirche* ed. Brooten/Greinacher pp. 212-234; 'Black Theology and Black Woman' in *Black Theology. A Documentary History* ed. Wilmore/Cone (New York 1979).

22. See especially Nelle Morton 'Towards a Whole Theology' in *Sexism in the 1970s* (Geneva 1975) pp. 56-65.

23. *Frau und Religion* ed. E. Moltmann-Wendel pp. 31ff.

24. From an unpublished poem 'My Mother Mary' by Joan Wyzenbeek read at the workshop 'Womanspirit Bonding' (Grailville 1982).

25. For a fuller development of such a feminist hermeneutics see my book *In Memory of Her. A Feminist Reconstruction of Christian Origins* (New York 1983) especially pp. 3-95, 343-351.

26. For such an approach see C. J. M. Halkes 'Feministische Theologie: Eine Zwischenbilanz' in *Frauen in der Männerkirche* ed. Brooten/Greinacher pp. 158-174 and the excellent new work of R. R. Ruether *Sexism and God-Talk. Toward a Feminist Theology* (Boston 1983).

27. From a poem entitled 'Women Behind Walls for the women in Cook County Jail and Dwight Prison' by Renny Golden in Golden/Collins *Struggle is a Name for Hope. Poetry* (Worker Writer Series 3) (Minneapolis 1982).

Joseph Bracken

An Example of Western Theology taking Modernity Seriously: 'Process Theology'

CONTEMPORARY MEN and women live in a rapidly changing world. At the same time, they consciously or unconsciously yearn for a world view or overarching frame of reference within which to assess the meaning and purpose of all these changes. Process theology, based on the philosophy of Alfred North Whitehead, is clearly an attempt to meet this felt need. Yet in its relatively brief history process thought has been sharply criticised by representatives of scholastic philosophy and theology on the grounds that Whitehead's conceptual scheme is seriously deficient as an explanation of reality and, *a fortiori*, as a philosophical framework for the articulation of Christian doctrine. In recent years, however, a more amiable dialogue between adherents of the two systems has taken place and the results are very promising. W. Norris Clarke, S.J., for example, long-time editor of the *International Philosophical Quarterly*, argues that 'process thought contains a number of basic insights that can and should be fruitfully assimilated by Christian theism', even as he maintains that process philosophy as a system 'is still in serious tension, if not incompatibility, with traditional Christian theism on several key points.'[1]

My intention is this article is, first, to offer a brief summary of what Fr. Clarke regards as the basic insights from process thought that should be assimilated into traditional Christian theism, and then to direct attention to those points where process theology seems to be incompatible with the traditional Christian doctrine of God. Perhaps a way can be found to circumvent those difficulties and thus to facilitate the acceptance of a modified form of process thought as a viable alternative to classical metaphysics for the articulation of Christian belief. For, as Clarke notes, 'it would be unwise . . . to lay down any unbridgeable incompatibilities of principle with future possible developments of the process stream of thought, since it itself is in full process of evolution, to which it is committed in principle.'[2]

Briefly, then, Clarke believes that classical theism must find a way to incorporate within the framework of Aristotelian-Thomistic metaphysics the presuppositions of process thought (a) that God is really related to the world of finite entities, (b) that he is contingently different, perhaps even mutable, because of what happens in the created order, and finally (c) that he is, accordingly, enriched in his own being by the response of his (rational) creatures to his loving activity in their midst. This can be done, argues Clarke, without repudiating the basic tenets of Aristotelian-Thomistic metaphysics,

40

provided that one distinguishes carefully between God's relational consciousness, i.e., the contents of the divine field of consciousness as related to creatures, and God's intrinsic inner being and perfection. For then one can say that in terms of God's inner perfection he 'does not become a more or less perfect being because of the love we return to him and the joy he experiences thereat (or its absence)'.[3] At the same time one can also urge that God in his intentional consciousness is deeply affected by the response of his creatures, i.e., experiences genuine joy or something like sadness in terms of his ongoing relationship with them.

Further details of Clarke's argument can be gathered from a close reading of his lecture; what has already been presented should make clear how traditional Christian theology can be enriched by the insights of process thought. What is to be said of the reverse procedure? Can, namely, the presuppositions of traditional Christian theism be brought into confrontation with Whitehead's system so as to bring about an expansion of the latter's categories and therewith an enrichment of his basic world view? Clarke points to two basic Christian beliefs that offer a direct challenge to Whitehead's philosophy: namely, that God is the transcendent Creator of heaven and earth, and that God is not just potentially infinite, as in Whitehead's system, but actually infinite vis-à-vis his creatures. I believe that with certain adjustments Whitehead's system can be employed to provide philosophical justification for these same Christian beliefs. Naturally, the way in which those beliefs are understood will inevitably be somewhat altered in keeping with Whitehead's process understanding of reality, but this in its own way should be an enrichment for Christian theology, i.e., still another way to explain the mysteries of the faith.

I will begin with the doctrine of God as Creator and address myself to what Clarke regards as the central problem in the Whiteheadian scheme if one is to retain belief in that same doctrine. According to Whitehead, God is an instantiation, albeit the primordial instantiation, of an ontological principle of being called Creativity.[4] From moment to moment Creativity thus sustains both God and the world of finite entities in existence. Yet, says Clarke, Creativity is then merely a principle for the multiplicity of beings (both finite and infinite); it does not account for the ontological unity of being traditionally grounded in God as the Supreme Being and Creator of all finite entities.[5] Thus, whereas traditional Christian theism unequivocally affirms the 'absolute priority of the One over the many',[6] Whitehead's metaphysics implicitly affirms the ontological priority of the many over the One.

To respond properly to this point, I will indeed have to enlarge upon Whitehead's explicit doctrine of Creativity somewhat, but, as I see it, in a way which is basically consistent with his overall world view and which likewise has the advantage of bringing his thought into dialogue both with classical metaphysics and with Martin Heidegger's critique of that same metaphysical tradition. Heidegger, it will be remembered, complained in *Identity and Difference* that classical ontology is really onto-theo-logy, i.e., reflection, less upon the nature of Being as such than upon the nature of the Supreme Being in its relation to its creatures.[7] Hence, concluded Heidegger, it is necessary to stop doing metaphysics in order to attend to the 'presencing' of Being in the beings of human experience.[8] My contention would be that Heidegger was fundamentally correct in his critique of classical metaphysics because philosophers of that persuasion, in their desire to ground the empirical Many in the transcendent One, have prematurely identified the unity of being with the Supreme Being, namely, God. The unity of being, on the contrary, should be provided by Being itself, understood as an ontological principle by which both God and the world of finite entities here and now exist. The unity of being is constituted then, not by the relation of all finite beings to God as the Supreme Being, but by the participation of all beings (including God as the Supreme Being) in a common act of existence. Moreover, thus understood, Being as an ontological principle of existence and activity for beings is remarkably akin to what Whitehead understands by Creativity.[9]

Whitehead, to be sure, in his discussion of Creativity, focuses his attention primarily on its role in the self-constitution of an actual entity, i.e., a momentary subject of experience which achieves a unification of all the factors in its world before it objectifies itself, transmits what it has become to its successor actual entity in the same process or 'route' of actual entities. Within this context, Creativity is 'that ultimate principle by which the many, which are the universe disjunctively, become the one actual occasion, which is the universe conjunctively'.[10] A few lines later he adds: in virtue of Creativity '[t]he many become one, and are increased by one'.[11] Passages such as these would naturally lead one to conclude that Clarke is correct in thinking that Creativity is simply a principle for the multiplicity and diversity of beings, hence that Whitehead's philosophy lacks an adequate principle for the unity of being.

In my judgment, the only way properly to respond to Clarke's critique is, as noted above, to make explicit what is implicit in Whitehead's understanding of Creativity. Whitehead holds, for example, that actual entities do not normally exist in isolation but instead are bound together in spatially and temporally organised 'societies' dominated by a 'common element of form'. This common element of form, moreover, is constituted from moment to moment by the way in which the member actual entities 'prehend' their unity as a group from a moment ago.[12] This too, without his calling attention to it, is the work of Creativity within Whitehead's scheme of things; that is, Creativity is responsible not only for the self-constitution of actual entities but also for the simultaneous constitution of the societies to which they belong. Creativity is, accordingly, not simply the principle of diversity within Whitehead's philosophy; it is likewise its principle of unity, albeit a dynamic principle of unity, in that the unity comes to be in and through the interrelatedness of diverse parts or members of a given society. Furthermore, when one takes into account Whitehead's dictum that every actual entity 'repeats in microcosm what the universe is in macrocosm',[13] hence that every actual entity has as part of its self-constitution now the 'common element of form' or basic configuration of the entire universe from a moment ago, then it follows that every actual entity, no matter how isolated it may seem to be from its contemporaries, as a matter of fact constitutes with them in virtue of the principle of Creativity an all-encompassing society of existents for that particular moment. Thus Creativity is unquestionably the ontological principle of unity within Whitehead's system as well as its concomitant principle of pluriformity and diversity. For in virtue of Creativity there is from moment to moment a universe, i.e., an ordered society of actual entities governed by a common element of form which is internal to the self-constitution of each actual entity.[14]

Admittedly, this is not the same type of unity which Clarke suggests is axiomatic for the history of Western philosophy since Plato: namely, the asymmetrical relationship of the Many to the One whereby the Many derive their unity not from their relationship to one another but from their common relationship to the transcendent One. Yet such a rudimentary paradigm shift in the understanding of the relationship of the One to the Many might be necessary in order to achieve the new, truly contemporary world view spoken of in the first paragraph of this article. In any case, it is ironic that Whitehead himself seems not to have grasped the full import of his own doctrine of Creativity as applied to the constitution of societies. That is, in his description of the God-world relationship in *Process and Reality*, Whitehead seems to have reverted to the classical paradigm for the relationship of the One to the Many; he seems, in other words, to have conceived the unity of the Many (the finite actual entities existing at any given moment) in terms of the superordinate One (God as the transcendent actual entity who prehends everything that exists in terms of his 'consequent nature', i.e., his own actuality at that particular moment).[15]

This is quite possibly due to the fact that Whitehead's concept of God was strictly monotheistic, not trinitarian. For a trinitarian understanding of God would have inevitably focused his attention on the role of Creativity in the constitution of societies. That is, if (as Whitehead urges) God is the primordial instantiation of Creativity, and if (in line with the trinitarian hypothesis) God is at any given moment not a single actual entity, but rather a society of three interrelated actual entities, then it seems to follow that the primary function of Creativity is to bring into existence societies of actual entities. Individual actual entities exist, in other words, not in and for themselves, but only as members of various societies (up to and including the all-comprehensive society of actual entities which constitutes the universe at any given moment). The three divine persons are no exception to this rule; instead, as we shall see below, by their innertrinitarian relationships to one another they provide the invariant pattern or structure for this same global society of all existents whatsoever.

Whitehead's categorical scheme, accordingly, with some modifications allows for a trinitarian understanding of God. Furthermore, the advantages of such a trinitarian understanding of God are quite considerable. First of all, thus revised, Whitehead's scheme is invulnerable to the critique of classical metaphysics made by Martin Heidegger. For ontology is no longer onto-theo-logy. The unity of being is not God but Being itself (i.e., Creativity), understood as a principle of existence and activity for all existents, including the three divine persons. But secondly and even more importantly for the interface between traditional Christian theism and process philosophy, a process-oriented doctrine of the Trinity makes possible a new understanding of God as Creator of heaven and earth and as truly infinite.

Clarke, for example, laments that the key metaphysical notion of participation is lacking in process thought.[16] Yet, according to the revised Whiteheadian scheme outlined above, whereby the three divine persons and all finite actual entities participate from moment to moment in a *common* act of existence, there is an even broader sense of participation than in classical metaphysics, where finite entities are said to participate in the fullness of the *divine* being. Furthermore, as I see it, the revised Whiteheadian scheme is logically neater, since it avoids the implicit ambiguity within classical metaphysics as to how finite beings can share in the plenitude of the divine being and yet exist in their own right. For, according to this approach, Creativity does not belong to the divine persons; rather, they are its primordial instantiations. That is, as I explain in detail elsewhere,[17] by their innertrinitarian relationships the divine persons structure the operation of Creativity even as they themselves exist in virtue of its life-giving power. Furthermore, they thereby set the conditions for the existence and activity of all finite actual entities. To be specific, just as the Father in the power of the Spirit continuously communicates being and life to the Son, so the Father is likewise the source of divine initial aims to all finite actual entities whereby, as Clarke notes,[18] they receive the power to exist and thus to respond to the Father's promptings in their regard. Moreover, just as the Son, again in the power of the Spirit, responds in love to the Father's initiative, so finite actual entities under the inspiration of the same Holy Spirit respond in a self-creative way to the Father's initial aims and thus align themselves more or less to the Son's response to the Father (thereby allowing for the possibility of both good and evil within creation). The result is a new understanding of the doctrine of creation and divine providence, according to which the divine persons and all their creatures jointly share in the adventure of existence but with the divine persons providing order and direction for the entire process.

The doctrine of the Trinity likewise seems to be the key to a new process-oriented understanding of divine infinity.[19] Within classical Whiteheadian metaphysics, God and the world are seen as polar opposites, each one limited and conditioned by the other.[20] Yet if it be admitted that God is triune, i.e., in Whiteheadian language a 'structured society' of three 'personally ordered societies' representing the divine persons,[21] then those same persons enjoy a life of their own over and above their relationship to their creatures. As noted above, they admit their creatures into the ongoing process of their own divine life but not in such a way as to alter its basic structure or the character of their basic relationship to one another. Hence their participation in the act of being or the power of Creativity is infinite, i.e., unlimited except in terms of their self-imposed innertrinitarian relationships. All creatures, on the other hand, participate in the act of being or the power of Creativity in a finite way because the manner of their participation is already fixed by the relationships of the three divine persons to one another. Thus all entities, both finite and infinite alike, participate in the ongoing process which is the act of being or the power of Creativity from moment to moment, but not all to the same degree or in the same way.

Admittedly, these remarks are still too sketchy and provisional to allow one to make a balanced judgment on the merits of process philosophy for the justification of traditional Christian beliefs. But at least they should open up for the reader the possibility of interpreting those same beliefs within a process frame of reference. As Clarke notes in the remark already cited, process thought itself 'is in full process of evolution, to which it is committed in principle'. Hence there is every reason to believe that with the passage of time process metaphysics will develop into a standard (if not the preferred) philosophical conceptuality for the articulation of Christian doctrine. The results for the Christian community should be in any event a new depth of understanding and a new breadth of symbolic reference in passing on the truth of the Gospel.

Notes

1. W. Norris Clarke, S.J. *The Philosophical Approach to God* (Winston-Salem, North Carolina 1979) p.66.

2. *Ibid.*

3. *Ibid.*, p. 92.

4. Alfred North Whitehead *Process and Reality* eds. D. Griffin and D. Sherburne (New York 1978) pp. 88 (135), 225 (344). N.B.: The number in parentheses corresponds to the 1929 edition of *Process and Reality*.

5. Clarke, the work cited in note 1, p. 72.

6. *Ibid.*, p. 74.

7. Martin Heidegger *Identity and Difference* tr. J. Stambaugh (New York 1969) p. 54 (*Identität und Differenz*, Pfullingen² 1957, p. 51).

8. See, e.g., 'The End of Philosophy and the Task of Thinking' *On Time and Being* tr. J. Stambaugh (New York 1972) pp. 55-73 ('Das Ende der Philosophie und die Aufgabe des Denkens' *Zur Sache des Denkens*, Tübingen² 1976, pp. 61-80).

9. See Clarke, the work cited in note 1, p. 83: 'The similarity [of Whiteheadian Creativity] with the Thomistic act of existence . . . is striking, though from other points of view the two notions are not identical.' It would be my contention, on the contrary, that they are simply two names for the same reality, although I readily concede to Clarke that Creativity and the act of existence play different roles in the philosophies of Whitehead and Aquinas respectively.

10. Whitehead, the work cited in note 4, p. 21 (31).

11. *Ibid.*, p. 21 (32).

12. *Ibid.*, p. 34 (50-51). See also my article 'Dependent Co-Origination, the Trinity and the God-World Relationship' available from the Center for Process Studies, Claremont, California (91711).

13. Whitehead, the work cited in note 4, p. 215 (327).

14. See on this point Ervin Laszlo *The Systems View of the World* (New York 1972) pp. 67-75. Laszlo's notion of a 'natural system', if applied to the universe as a whole, somewhat resembles my conception here of an all-embracing Whiteheadian 'society'.

15. Whitehead, the work cited in note 4, pp. 344-351 (523-33).

16. Clarke, the work cited in note 1, pp. 98-99.

17. See 'Process Philosophy and Trinitarian Theology—II' in *Process Studies* 11 (1981) pp. 85-91; see also a forthcoming article on the same topic in the *Journal of Religion* (April, 1984).

18. Clarke, the work cited in note 1, pp. 78-83.

19. *Ibid.*, p. 102.

20. See Whitehead, the work cited in note 4, p. 348 (528).

21. See my article 'Process Philosophy and Trinitarian Theology' in *Process Studies* 8 (1978) pp. 224-226.

Meinrad Hegba

From the Generalisation of one Triumphant Particular to the Search for True Universality

INTRODUCTION

THERE IS a way of talking about the unity and the universality of the Church which has more to do with partisan ideology than objectivity. When I say, 'I believe in the one, universal Church', what unity and universality am I talking about?

It is an obvious fact that there are many historical christianities, institutionalised in hundreds of independent churches, Catholic, Orthodox and Protestant. Most of these christianities are organised in coherent, solid systems, each integrating in its own way the contribution of European or Asian paganism, Judaism or the New Testament. The result is several competing syntheses, divergent and antithetical, but now substituting peaceful coexistence, if not attempts at ecumenical convergence, for the Manichean self-righteousness common only a short time ago, which itself was an advance on the barbarism of the wars of religion. But there is no doctrinal synthesis at the level of world Christianity. In other words, a universal Christian language does not yet exist. At the very most, it is in the process of being formed. Even if it did exist among the present denominational churches, it would be no more than a universality of a very special kind. The majority of the human race is outside the Church of Christ: Moslems, Jews, Buddhists, followers of various natural religions, atheists, those with no interest in any religion. What sort of universality is this, which includes no more than a small part of the totality?

Let us take the point a little further. If one day the proportions were reversed, and practically the whole of humankind entered the church, as long the theological expression and the juridical and disciplinary organisation continued to be determined by the West, by Greco-Byzantinism and the Slav world, we would still not have a genuine universality, but a precarious particular seeking in its triumph to impose itself illegitimately as a universal. So when I say, 'I believe in the universal Church,' I mean to confess my faith in the mustard seed sown by Christ and destined to grow to match the human race and history. I believe in a Church which has a universal vocation but which will probably remain until the parousia the 'remnant', condemned for ever to a modest existence, once it has recovered from the inflating effect of triumphalist statistics and the utopian hope of conquering the whole of humanity and enclosing it in a visible institution, a theocratic and authoritarian super-state.

46

1. THE PARTICULARISM OF THE KATHOLIKÉ

(a) The universality of the rule of faith

According to St Paul, there is but 'one Lord, one faith, one baptism' (Eph. 4:5). Consequently the formulation of dogmatic statements cannot be left to individual initiative; unity of meaning and universality of destination are conveivable only if an obligatory norm of reference is accepted, the rule of faith defined and proposed by the *magisterium*. The procedures for this formulation and definition are variable, and there could be endless discussion about the force of different propositions or the mutual dependence of the various bodies involved in the formulation; pope, councils, bishops and theologians.

(b) The expression of the rule: the stumbling block

The principle of the necessity and the existence of a common rule of faith is beyond discussion. It was stressed with unusual force by Pope Paul VI in Kampala when he spoke to the Symposium of the Episcopal Conferences of Africa and Madagascar (SCEAM) in 1969. The pope said that when the burning question was asked, whether the faith in Africa should be Latin, Greek or African, the answer was that it should be African. But, said the pope, it should first of all be Catholic, the same as the faith professed by the apostles, the martyrs, the early fathers and the missionaries. The pope continued:

> You know that the Church is particularly strict, even conservative on this point. To ensure that the message of revealed teaching is not altered, the Church has enshrined its treasure of truth in certain conceptual and verbal formulas. Even if these formulas are sometimes difficult, the Church obliges us to preserve them literally: we are not the inventors but the guardians of our faith.[1]

Commentators think that the pope was here referring to controversies buffeting the Catholic fortress at the time. In 1965, in the encyclical *Mysterium Fidei*, he had already insisted on the permanent suitability of the ancient dogmatic formulations to express the Catholic faith: there was no need to replace 'transubstantiation' by 'transsignification'. Later, in 1973, the Congregation for the Doctrine of the Faith published the declaration *Mysterium Ecclesiae*, which was intended to clarify the true Catholic conception of the development of dogma. The declaration was directed at certain champions of the 'inculturation' of the language of faith, in other words, of its translation into terms of contemporary European culture in order to make it intelligible to people of the modern West.

This problem is extremely complex. Anyone can appreciate the reluctance of a pope to declare statements of the faith solemnly defined by general councils or popes outdated, but it is equally clear that theologians who are also pastors are also anguished by the increasing indifference of the European and American intelligentsia to a Christian language which means absolutely nothing to them. Such people are put off by the jargon of Aristotelian and Thomistic philosophy or the Byzantian subtleties of Nicea or Chalcedon. According to Paul VI, there can be no tampering with terms such as '*ousia*, *homoousios*, "nature", "person", "substance", "accident"', because they embody the quintessence of revealed truth. Hans Küng, Edward Schillebeeckx and others, however, are undertaking an updating of concepts and words, in their view an essential prerequisite for fidelity to the meaning of the formulations of the faith. The pope demands an irrevocable adherence to a proposition immutable even in its form; the theologians believe that no human expression, biblical or dogmatic, can adequately convey divine

truth. It expresses something of it, but it is always limited by its geographical, ideological, philosophical, cultural and temporal conditioning. Once outside this well-defined
framework, the language one uses needs to be re-examined. Obvious!

But if so many Western Christians are so ill at ease in a conceptual universe which is
nevertheless theirs, what must be the feelings of so many Africans and others, condemned to become Western in order to be saved?

(c) The Western-Eastern monopoly of the philosophical substratum of the faith

Even at the dawn of the third millennium, the attitude of official Christianity remains
ambivalent: in words very universalist, in practice it is dominated by a triumphant and
intransigent particularism. Forced judaisation was abolished at the order of the holy
Spirit and the apostles; who will save us from philosophical, juridical and cultural
Westernisation, erected into the providential path towards salvation in Jesus Christ? Not
Jesus the Christ himself, not his companions, not even Paul and Luke, hellenists to some
extent though they were, judged it essential to formulate Christian teaching in the
language of Greek philosophy. Today, however, even a Jew coming to Christianity has
to abandon the rabbinic culture in which the New Testament is bathed and adopt
Western thought. The fathers worked out their theology primarily in terms of neo-
Platonic philosophy. St Thomas used Aristotelianism. Councils and popes had but to
follow a path already outlined. Ever after the Catholic faith has been expressed in Greek
and scholastic terms, and apart from those its orthodoxy is not guaranteed. On their side
Protestants express themselves mainly in Germanic philosophies, and Hegel's dialectic
was the tool of the great theologian Karl Barth. The result is that, apart from the raw
New Testament data, the Christian faith is required to be expressed in Western philosophical concepts. Can God really have conducted the mass of our fellow Christians to
mechanical repetition of words and phrases alien to their conceptual universe which
have to be understood on their behalf by deculturalised Westernised theologians? Is this
good news?

(d) Western culture, the norm of doctrinal development

Let us take the case of marriage. The conception of the sacrament of marriage in
the Catholic church has undergone a long evolution under the exclusive influence of
the development of European and general Western culture—apart, of course, from the
assistance of the holy Spirit. The contrast here is striking. The Roman church in the
European world adapted to the marriage laws and customs of nations, wisely following
the rule of tolerance and gradualism over the centuries. In Black Africa it has shown
itself intolerant, rigid and uncompromising, and refused to take into account the
institutions of our ancestors.

Europe. For a long time engagement was regarded as the beginning of marriage, a
view which may have been taken over from Jewish law.[2] Conjugal relations could begin
at any point, because the canonical form (the exchange of consent before an official
representative of the Church) did not become obligatory until 1563, with the council of
Trent's decree *Tametsi*. And *Tametsi* remained a dead letter for more than three
centuries, and was not really applied until the appearance of the Holy Office decree *Ne
temere* in 1908. Were the 'clandestine marriages' of this period all void?

According to Edward Schillebeeckx, the Church, especially in Germany, did not
always treat the personal consent of the two parties, especially of the woman, as a
condition of the validity of the sacrament.[3]

Moreover, the end of marriage was at first solely the procreation of children. St
Augustine and other fathers, influenced by a whole Orphic tradition which came down

to them through Plato, Diogenes, Philo of Alexandria and neo-Platonism, are the main sources of the guilt complex which makes any discussion of sex in the Catholic Church very tense. St Thomas Aquinas teaches that conjugal relations are tainted with sin the moment the couple seek pleasure apart from procreation.[4] Pius XI, however, in *Casti Connubii* (1930), admits a distinction between the primary end (procreation and education) and a secondary end (mutual love and the avoidance of concupiscence). With the progress of psychology and above all of psychoanalysis, which have transformed Western attitudes to sex, the Church finally declared, through the mouth of Pius XII, that there was no sin, not even venial, in the proper enjoyment of conjugal relations. It is true that Paul VI and John-Paul II have resolutely opposed the wave of hedonism which is sweeping over the world, condemning with laudable stubbornness practices such as contraception, abortion, divorce and homosexuality which accommodating theologians have not hesitated to defend. Nevertheless, when one looks at the distance travelled by the *magisterium* itself, would it not be reasonable to suggest, with Fr. E. Hillman, that if a nuclear war drastically reduced the number of men in the West, there would be theologians to appeal to the Bible in defence of the legitimacy of polygamy?[5]

*Africa.*Traditional African marriage was condemned by the missionaries. The practice here was that the engaged couple became man and wife gradually, as the dowry was paid and agreement between the families developed.

The range of permitted degrees of affinity varies in different nations. The Church first admitted all the European systems and then, having tried in vain to impose the Roman system in the seventh century, finally incorporated the German system into canon law in 1065. Fr. Van Driessche asks why the Africans were not allowed to keep their system.[6]

The Church approached polygamous marriage brutally, citing New Testament texts the probative force of which is still not seen by the Western exegetes most contemptuous of 'these primitive customs'.[7] Paul III, in the Apostolic Constitution *Altitudo* (1537), citing I Cor. 7:12, decided that if a polygamous man, after his conversion, could not remember which of his wives was the first, he could be baptised with the wife of his choice. Extending still further the Pauline privilege, which by now had become Petrine, St Pius V, in 1571, decided, in the Apostolic Constitution *Romani Pontificis*, that, even if later the man with the short memory remembered that another wife had been the first, the 'Christian marriage' which had replaced the natural marriage by breaking it in a unilateral divorce should be maintained. Bogus amnesiacs took the opportunity to rejuvenate their households, and, in order to save their precious male souls for eternity, the 'supernumerary wives' were condemned to prostitution or another polygamous union. Why could tolerance and gradualism not have been employed in Africa too? Because doctrinal development is a function of a single variable, the development of the Western conscience.

2. TOWARDS AN ADULT AFRICAN CHRISTIANITY

It is sometimes said that Africans are poor relations in the Church. That is true, and in token of it the part of this article devoted to them will be very short. To be accurate, it should be said that they are regarded as children at the breast or still fed on pap, that is, food pre-digested by others (1 Cor. 3:2; Heb. 5:12-14).

(a) The infantile age of faith

It is inevitable that the community which receives the faith should go through a longer or shorter period of imitation. In this period the profession of faith is reduced to the correct recitation of formulas learnt by heart, decorated with foreign terms (Greek,

Latin, French, English, Spanish, etc.). Of course, this verbal recitation is based on a vague adherence to the word of God taught by the Church. This period corresponds on the whole to the first proclamation of the word and the first stage of catechesis. It is impossible to determine its length in advance. Too often it is prolonged indefinitely, and catechetical mimicry is refined into a higher form in clerical training. At the beginning faculties of theology are colleges of assimilation in which native students are drilled in the rudiments of scholastic philosophy and Thomism among Catholics, and in another European philosophy and one of the Protestant theologies among our separated brethren. There are very few individuals with enough personality to escape the moulding which tends to turn them into simple purveyors of an off-the-peg Christianity, bishops and priests more Catholic than the pope and pastors more Protestant than Luther and Calvin, who regard it as their duty to perpetuate the religious infantilism of their fellows in the name of fidelity and unity.

(b) Growth through the inculturation of theology

What is really needed is growth in the faith, personal commitment to Jesus Christ at a level deeper than that of the Samaritan woman (John 4:42). Christ has to become incarnate in every culture, to be confessed in all languages, that is, in all forms of speech and thought, all moral traditions. So many subjects have been left untouched by the classical theologies, from disdain or cowardice; we must tackle them ourselves in full Gospel freedom. These questions include the following: What justifies our Christian existence? How should we judge in the light of revelation a world order which means for us a position of structural subjection, economic, political, cultural and religious? What does Jesus Christ—not Christian civilisation—think of our ancestral religions and our social institutions? What light does the Gospel throw on the world of witchcraft and spells, and what encouragement may we look for from Jesus Christ's powerful word for healing, once foreign elucubrations on animism and primitivism have been demystified? What can we gain from the interpretations of Christianity put forward by the various independent churches? There are other subjects too of far greater urgency for us than the construction of learned theologies.

In any case, we are no longer at the stage of the first formulation of theories; there has been any number of articles and books.[8] What is a serious problem for us, though, is that of theological language or theological expression. Mgr. A. Sanon and Fr. Bimwenyi Kweshi, among others, have demonstrated that it is the whole Christian community responding to the message of Christ which does theology, in other words, which reacts vitally to that message and takes a position with regard to Christ, who bursts into their society. The theological professionals may then have a role to play in criticising and organising this disparate material, made up of liturgical songs and attitudes, a greater or lesser degree of syncretism between the Gospel and elements drawn from traditional religions. This implies that the theologians submit to the assessment of the members of the community the interpretation of the Gospel message they attribute to the community, and therefore that they speak a language which is accessible to the people, as well as to their foreign colleagues. That language cannot be scholastic, Hegelian or Heideggerian. What is to be done? The only solution is to have recourse to the instruments of communication provided by the languages developed by others, but with flexibility, and occasionally giving their concepts and terms a comprehension and extension corresponding to the demands of our own semantic universe.

The Catholic hierarchy of Africa and Madagascar, on the whole, encourages the enterprise of theological inculturation. This is the message, for example of the declaration issued by the Symposium of Episcopal Conferences of Africa and Madagascar (SCEAM) after the synod of bishops held in Rome in October 1974.

In 1977 the Abidjan Colloquium launched the idea of holding an African council, with no fixed date or agenda, to stimulate the thinking of the African churches and encourage them to make explicit their commitment to Christ. Encouraged by various bishops, eminent African lay people, including the late lamented Alioune Diop, president of the Societé Africaine de Culture, went to share the idea with Paul VI, who did not discourage them. In its turn, the important episcopal conference of Zaïre, consisting of almost 50 bishops, discussed the matter with John-Paul II in Kinshasa. The pope is said to have been broadly sympathetic. However, it must be admitted that most of our bishops made no response to the Abidjan appeal. This prompted these African theologians, under the aegis of the Société Africaine de Culture, to use the power of the media to relaunch the idea from the heart of Europe. During their stay in France and Belgium they received messages of encouragement from SCEAM officials. But, as usual, the most insidious threats against African initiatives came from the Africans themselves, from those native structures admirably trained to break any attempt among their compatriots to strike out on new paths. Foreign journalists gave prominence to the sharp criticisms of some of our bishops and priests, who challenged the representativity of the three council pilgrims, or the opportunities of launching the appeal from European soil. When a French theologian-journalist asked us point-blank, 'Which of your bishops are against the project?', the biting reply was: 'Those who have chosen foreigners as theological advisors in preference to Africans!'

CONCLUSION

The reason for the Accra Colloquium's advocacy of a new theological method, departing from the principles of the classical theologies, is that the classical theologies are particularist. They are imprisoned in the ghetto of the European philosophical and cultural world, in a false universal which is really no more than a random but victorious particular. Western philosophers and theologians believe that it is the flexibility and rigour of this way of thought which have enabled it to triumph over all others. Some hold, with the scholastics, that they have produced the *philosophia perennia*, the substratum of human thought in general. Others, more modern in their outlook, stress the possibilities of a language and way of thought which made possible the flowering of science and technology. But beneath all the exaggeration what is being discussed is no more than a human philosophy. This has been clearly illustrated by the incredible identification of doctrinal development with the development of the European mind. The classical theologies are not sufficiently open to deal with the questions we face. What we want to do is to make our modest contribution to the coming of a genuinely universal Church. Peter, the first pope, left us the brave example of conversion from a judaising Christianity to Christianity pure and simple (Acts 10-11). The holy Spirit can bring about the same conversion in those who are imposing a Westernising or Easternising Christianity on the whole world. If those in power allow themselves to be converted, the *katholikē* will have set out on the path to becoming what it is, genuinely universal.

Translated by Francis McDonagh

Notes

1. AAS, 30 Sept. 1969, pp. 576ff.
2. G. H. Joyce *Christian Marriage* (London 1948).

3. *Marriage, Secular Reality and Saving Mystery* (London 1965) pp. 33ff.

4. ST 1a. q. 98, 3; Suppl. 49, 6.

5. E. Hillman *Polygamy Reconsidered* (New York 1965) p. 12.

6. *L'Empêchement de parenté en droit coutumier africain* (Paris 1959) pp. 113ff., 271.

7. Hillman, the work cited in note 5, pp. 139-169. The author surveys the views of reputed Catholic and Protestant exegetes and theologians on the texts adduced to condemn what he calls 'the plural marriage'.

8. *Telema* (Kinshasa), *Bulletin de l'AOTA* (Kinshasa) and *Africa Theological Journal* (Dar es Salaam), give good bibliographies.

PART III

The Plurality of Theologies as a Theological Problem

Ernst Käsemann

Differences and Unity in the New Testament

BOTH HISTORICALLY and theologically, the unity of the New Testament is a problem. Over a period of about a hundred years, and in different regions, a conglomerate of different literary genres and theological conceptions grew up, which give us highly fragmentary information about the earliest years of Christian history. Important events have acquired a legendary colouring, are blurred, allusive, or have been transmitted from a one-sided viewpoint. Important people are hardly more than names to us. The organisation of the individual churches—which were at most linked together in provinces—differed by tradition, through the possibilities open to them, and because of local needs. An over-riding hierarchical order only prevailed after Enthusiasm had to be repulsed. From the very beginning there were non-conformists, and by no means merely on the periphery. We generally hear about everyday conditions and forms of worship only when these led to controversy.

The discontinuity in the historical development is patent. Everywhere critical reconstruction runs up against gaps and an almost inconceivable diversity; and the four canonical Gospels can only be the indication of a wider tradition now lost to us. Their factual differences and contradictions cannot be harmonised. What seems even more surprising is that an 'apostolic' heritage in the strict sense has come down to us only from Paul and his followers, although pseudepigrapha conceal this. There is no doubt that here the heretic Marcion had a finger in the pie. But it is impossible to be sure whether his 'canon' is a selection from texts used in the worship of the major churches, or whether it was explained in a 'catholicised' sense by texts of this kind. At all events, the New Testament in its present form did not emerge without internal conflicts and political compromises in the Church. Here at least, 'Believed everywhere, always, by everyone' is not an appropriate slogan. Theologically, preference might well be given to some texts which remained apocryphal, rather than to the alleged epistles of James or II Peter.

I am saying this first of all in order to show that even biblical history is not logically calculable, and was not an organic growth. Dogmatic postulates cannot gloss over the fact that much of this history was lost, forgotten or suppressed, or remained inconsistent and contradictory. Uniformity can only exist when social conditions are violated, and if one shuts one's eyes to the protean wealth of reality—to the point of stupidity or perhaps even pious fraud. Unity in the human sphere—which means in the Christian sphere too—can only be solidarity in difference. But even in the New Testament this solidarity

55

is not as general as apologetics would like to suggest. Truth on earth is always bound to the dimensions of space and time, and to the *kairos*—the particular and appropriate time—of its witnesses and opponents. It has to be seen in perspective, in changing contexts and in specific relations. Truth is never objectively and permanently verifiable: its atmosphere is always dimmed; the subjectivity of the proclaimer must always be remembered. The Gospel can be frozen into permanence only if it is distorted. The incarnation of the Word involves a continually new experience of that Word; and in the Church's history this is reflected through new theological beginnings.

The fundamental confession of the Christian faith in 1 Cor. 15:3ff. is probably the formulation of catechetical baptismal tradition: 'He was seen (as the One who had been raised).' We have to view the whole New Testament as the interpretation of this declaration for each new generation. In its variations, the unity of the Church, as the ambassador of the Gospel, is proclaimed for changing times, regions and questions. The very fact that the event of the resurrection is not as such described, shows that originally the whole stress lay on the manifestation of the Christ already exalted—the Christ who calls his church to its mission, as in Matt. 28:18ff. It is in accordance with this that here the concern is not Jesus' individual destiny and the physical reality of the One risen from the tomb (unlike the gospel stories, which tell how the raised Jesus ate and drank with his disciples). Perhaps this explains the almost incomprehensible riddle that in the gospels neither James nor the 500 brethren appear as Easter witnesses; that Peter's primacy is only indistinctly derived from his fundamental encounter with the exalted Jesus; and that preference is given to legendary accounts. For the later Church, the historically unquestionable facts in 1 Cor. 15 may not have been clearly enough differentiated from visionary experiences. Their interest was already no longer constitutively the break-in of the End-time initiated by Jesus' resurrection—an expectation which appears liturgically in Rom. 1:3f. or Col. 1:18 and 1 Tim. 3:16, and which inspires Paul in 1. Cor. 15:25 to interpret the Easter Gospel as: 'He must reign until he has put all his enemies under his feet.' Here what is proclaimed is the opened heavens and the new earth, initiated in the Church which lives from the divine peace, so that its members, like the angels, stand before the face of God' and are sent into all the world as witnesses of the final creation. Here the Easter faith takes its bearings from the kingdom of the End-time. The exalted Lord gives this kingdom its character, and he for his part takes his definition solely from that kingdom. We have to analyse Early Christian history from the shifts in this correlation, if we want to comprehend its different phases.

Paul's view unmistakeably already reflects an advanced stage. The first Christians interpreted Easter in the context of God's covenant with Israel, which will be renewed with the appearance of the Messiah and the public manifestation of his glory. Now the disciples are sent forth to gather the restored people of the twelve tribes, as the kingdom of the Messiah. Jesus himself fulfilled the law of Moses 'in spirit and in truth', manifesting the dawn of the era of salvation with 'signs and wonders'. Now he leaves his disciples 'the new law', this time initiated through 'beatitudes', bringing the old into line with the perfect commandment of love, and hence giving it a new, radical force. The 'holy remnant' calls for the conversion of the whole of Israel and waits in suffering discipleship for the second coming of the Son of man, and the consummation it will bring.

But soon after Easter the organisation of the Church already threatened to break apart. The disciples grouped round Peter and the twelve were largely Palestinian in origin; whereas the 'offspring' of the Jewish dispersion gathered round the Seven, especially Stephen. Problems about the diaconate may have helped to cause the division. But the trial of Stephen, with the probably accurate indictment, points to essential theological differences. The 'hellenists'—like the Epistle to the Hebrews later—declared that the ritual law of the old covenant had been superseded. The exalted Lord, who had given them his Spirit, was more than temple or Torah. For the first time in the history of the Church, the watchwords 'Christ alone' and 'by faith alone' became the subject of dispute. It is significant that the group round James was not affected by the subsequent persecution by the Jews. For this group, the Church was Judaism with faith in the Messiah who had come. The Gentiles had access to it only by way of circumcision and the acceptance of the law. That is to say, it was only open to proselytes. The 'hellenists', in contrast, defined ecclesiology radically in terms of Christology: Jesus' exaltation is the dawn of the kingdom to which not only Israel and the proselytes have been invited; as the Old Testament promises, the God-fearing Gentiles too will journey there. The story of Pentecost is based on the Jewish legend that the sound of the Torah echoed forth from Sinai to all nations; and so the Spirit of the End-time leads away from the national ghetto into a new creation. As this new creation, the whole inhabited earth will now be the goal and upholder of the new covenant. After Easter, the mission to the Gentiles is the distinguishing mark of the Church.

A heavy price had to be paid for this insight. We can see this from what happened to Peter. According to the Book of Acts, the prince of the apostles was basically prepared to take the new direction. Acts 10, with the story of the converted centurion, Cornelius—and especially the vision interwoven in 10:9ff.—may reflect the break-through. But with this Peter's authority began to decline. In the council of the apostles his attitude was practically opposed by Jewish Christians who were strict observers of the law. The main role had already fallen to James, the Lord's brother, who now also took over leadership of the church in Jerusalem. In 1 Cor. 9:5 we already hear of Peter as missionary, supported by his wife, to whom the women's quarters were more accessible. In Antioch Peter is then watched by spies from James's party, and is apparently accused of breaking the law because he eats with Gentile Christians. Evidently he is unable to get his way in the dispute and, together with Barnabas, withdraws from these meals. Paul is exceedingly angry with him and from then on conspicuously ceases to mention Antioch at all, but carries on his own mission. The period of compromise between the church in Jerusalem—with its offshoot in Antioch?—and the increasingly independent Gentile church was approaching its end. Even the collections taken up for the earliest Christian congregation, which Paul vigorously pursued (in spite of his doubts about their success, according to Rom. 15:25ff.) hardly did anything to change this. The way was paved for the first schism in the Church's history, as Jerusalem lost control over the continually growing Gentile church. Romans 11:13ff. and Ephesians 2:11ff. indicate that the original Church was being forced out of the centre. After becoming a heretical sect, Jewish Christianity was finally swamped by Islam. But Peter was probably martyred in Rome as exile. It was only his tomb which reinstated him. The apostolic succession is a strange affair.

The separation from Jerusalem, however, had momentous consequences for the Gentile church as well, long before the Jewish inheritance withered, dogmatically speaking, under the weight of Greek philosophy. 1 Corinthians provides the clearest evidence that mission also led the Church into the surrounding field of the hellenistic mystery religions, and that new converts could sometimes interpret Christianity as a variant of these mysteries. Ever since, asceticism, mysticism, ecstasy, and finally attempts at emancipation have continually put their stamp on the Church in its existing form. We must confine ourselves to a few examples from the wealth of the detailed material. The young Church was dominated by Enthusiasm. For the individual, the break-in of the heavenly kingdom into earthly life took place in baptism, which was interpreted as an initiation rite. Through baptism, the individual was interpenetrated by the Spirit, as the power of the resurrection. So that even liturgical texts like Col. 1:13—not merely the heretics in 2 Tim. 2:18—maintain that resurrection and participation in heavenly existence have already come about. This was probably the reason why the Corinthian Enthusiasts declared that the future resurrection was unnecessary. The bodily garment fell away in death. This was the only consummation still to come. The Eucharist was the proleptic celebration of the banquet of the blessed. Speaking with tongues was particularly esteemed because it echoed the language of the angels. The body of Christ was the counter-world in which earthly ordinances no longer restricted complete liberty and equality. There were no misgivings about visiting friends in heathen temples; Christians did not even shrink from the meat used for sacrifices there.

'All things are yours': In 1 Cor. 3:22f. Paul picks up the slogan of the men and women intoxicated by their freedom. At the same time he confronts them inflexibly with the impassable barrier: 'But you are Christ's.' In their absorption with the kingdom of heaven, they are paying too little attention to the Lord and hence, inevitably, to the brethren and the world too. This is the very heartbeat of Pauline theology. For us today this theology may sometimes seem alien, in the depth of its reflection and in the typically Jewish nature of its thinking and its argumentation. But in content it rightly occupies the very centre of the canon. Fresh and highly individual as it is—a complex of many individual comments on contemporary issues—Paul's theology is the foundation of the whole of Western dogmatics. But it also mediates between the opposing positions which threatened to break asunder during the apostle's lifetime. Even he did not succeed in holding together as organisation what clashed so fiercely at the time, although he tried to do so until the day of his death. But theologically he pointed unremittingly towards the centre from which unity in difference could be achieved. He radicalised the message of the 'hellenists' by making their 'Christ alone' point to Jesus' cross, and gave a sharper edge to their 'by faith alone' through his thesis about the justification of the godless.

This thesis is not just the speculation of a wild extremist (although that is the general opinion in the churches). On the contrary: it is the simple expression of the apostolic work which in the Gospel brings the Gentiles the salvation which is not solely for the pious. Paul talks about justification because the Creator has a claim to all his creatures; and because the lost, the rebellious and the sinful only find their way back to the heavenly Father who has created them, and to their eternal salvation, when they again learn to live from *his* claims and *his* sovereignty, instead of serving the principalities and powers of this world. The only paradoxical thing about this message is that God in the last days has manifested his claim to those he has created on the cross on Golgatha, founding our salvation on the lordship of the crucified Christ. It is in that lordship— which in concrete terms means in the body of Christ—that salvation is preserved and consummated. But underlying the paradox is the insight that the sinner can be conquered only through love. Superior power would drive him into defiance or despair. The dying Jesus becomes our brother, and brings us into the kingdom of grace instead of fear, liberated from the demons of self-will, possession and the inhumanity that springs from these. He shows us the image of the Father, who has not given us up and who humbles himself to our level; and at the same time he shows us our own true image, cleansed from illusion. He shows it too to the people who consider themselves devout, taking the example of the Jews faithful to the law, who help to set up Christ's cross and acclaim it. The people who want to impress God with their achievements, and to save themselves by their good works are godless too. The crucified Jesus also sets aside the law between God and man, between Jews and Gentiles, where this makes our salvation depend on what we do ourselves. Lovingly, he joins together everything that is divided, and his sovereignty is a call solely to the mutual service of love. One must ask whether the will and work of the Nazarene have ever been more fittingly interpreted than by Paul, who never saw the earthly Jesus and who, when he wants to characterise the lordship of the Christ who was raised, concentrates wholly on Christ crucified. This very concentration prevents the bringer of salvation from being reduced to a model for moral behaviour. All history can now be interpreted as time under the sign of the crucified Lord and his claim to every human being. 'Christ must reign' is its hidden centre and its End-time goal.

It is not by chance that Pauline theology develops more strongly than the other New Testament writings a firmly outlined doctrine of man, letting this reflect what universally determines salvation history and the history of the world. In this way the Jewish message about the covenant with Israel is extended to the whole of creation. God does not create a ghetto of people with a pious outlook; his grace confers no privileges. Christian theology is ecumenically orientated or it is not evangelical. But it is not, either, one of the ideologies into which churches so often take flight. It has to do with reality, which means the everyday life of every individual. Paul's realism distinguishes him from the Enthusiasts, although he breathes the same air. Salvation is present. It blesses and claims both world and individual. Yet the everyday Christian life is resistance against enticing and threatening demonic powers. Christ rules; but God still has to become all in all. Baptism confers grace; the Eucharist confirms the grace conferred. But according to 1 Cor. 10:1-13 neither of them guarantees earthly security. Anyone who was incorporated in Christ's body can still deny the Lord and the brethren. Earthly discipleship is bodily discipleship, in communication and confrontation.

This emerges most forcibly in Paul's doctrine of the charismata. With ecumenical breadth and yet with individual reference, this teaches believers to see the Church as the general priesthood of all believers in everyday life. Every Christian is personally called, endowed and sent forth by his Lord, in order, as it were, to keep the image of that Lord on earth alive, provocative, unmistakeable. Here there is neither privilege nor passivity. Everyone is in his own way irreplaceable. In his own place he is bearer of the Word and Christ's representative in the only succession that can truly be called apostolic, and in the office sacramentally established through baptism—the office to which all other offices merely give concrete form. Here the Church is determined by Christology. This must neither be relativised nor reversed.

In practice, this theology has always been accepted only at times of crisis and in criticism of existing conditions. To later believers (as 2 Peter 3:16 frankly says) its way of thinking seemed too complicated, its radicalism too dangerous, its interest in organisation too feeble. This was so even where the apostle's heritage was not completely forgotten or suppressed by rampant Enthusiasm, Jewish-Christian traditions and trends towards conciliation between the centres of the major churches. Paul's theology was ironed out and moralised in the interests of pious domesticity. 'The family of God' was shielded by the protective wall of ordination, presbytery and monarchical episcopacy, on the Jewish-Christian model. This is clearly brought out in the pastoral epistles. Stress is now, not on the justification of the godless, but on ecclesiology, on which—in Ephesians—a separate theological treatise is devoted. The new perspective of thought and action is the fostering and instruction of the faithful. A new religion is formed.

We find the beginnings of this process in Luke's historical writings. Brief collections of the sayings of miracles of Jesus, accounts of the passion, the early Church and the beginnings of mission had already existed earlier. They are sometimes even still identifiable as sources of New Testament tests. So the remembrance of historical events was already cultivated in the earliest congregation, even if the norms of modern tradition, or even Greek historiography, did not generally prevail. Legendary expansion is indisputable. Edification and liturgical interests were motive forces. Luke, on the other hand, has a firm and comprehensive programme which he carries out with the zeal of the ardent collector, a rhetorical skill unequalled in the New Testament, and an admirable logic of composition. He recapitulates Christian salvation history from the birth of John the Baptist to the arrival of the Gospel in Rome, as the centre of the world. It is important to see that this historical concept manifests a whole particular theology. Here the early Church's ardent expectation of the Lord's imminent coming, and the Enthusiastic proclamation of present, visible consummation are mentioned only incidentally. It is already typical that in this concept Jesus' earthly life inevitably becomes the pre-history of the lordship of the Spirit in the era of the missionary church; that Jesus himself becomes the initiator and founder of the Christianity which conquers the world; and that this has to be viewed as fulfilling and superseding God's way of salvation with Israel. More surprising than this, the Church represents the prolongation of revelation. This makes the exalted Jesus the heavenly conductor, as it were, in the realisation of the plan of salvation.

The miracle accounts and surprising interventions of the Spirit cannot hide the fact that this is the outline of a universal historical development which runs straight according to the intentions of providence, in spite of unavoidable incidents and even martyrdoms. The skilful reduction to the life of the early Christian community, and the implementation through Paul (as delegated pioneer of the world-wide Church) of the missionary programme resolved upon at the council of the apostles, is of impressive power; no less so are the addresses in Acts, with their adaptation to the particular situation; while the wealth of illustrative scenes depict with the simplicity of genius the inexorably victorious progress of the Gospel. Here, as points of orientation, we are given facts which, though they are supernaturally initiated, are firmly anchored in earthly happening. Psychological intuition, a largely stylised language (especially imitative of the Old Testament) and moral edification in the style of legends of the saints, all intensify the effect for listeners who are to be enlisted for the great mission of Christianity. Down to the present day, Acts still presents a fascinating and unsurpassed picture, in all its original colours, of the missionary propaganda of the triumphant Church.

The theology of the first three ('synoptic') gospels is the most difficult question. We seldom come upon indubitably authentic material about Jesus. There are no eye-witness accounts, and the text is not based on first-hand sources. Instead the evangelists have threaded together a multiplicity of fragments of the most varying origin as best they could. We cannot, therefore, expect a unified theology. Every fragment must be considered separately for its viewpoint, original context, the changes it has undergone during transmission, and its relation to today's circumstances. We must also remember that, as well as the traditions about the passion and Easter, the evangelists already had at their disposal short liturgical formulas (for example the Lord's Prayer or the eucharistic words), collections of miracle stories, and the beginnings of an order for the Church's life. Matthew and Luke also present stories about Jesus' birth and childhood, but have above all used the same collections of sayings. Selection, specific information and the method of using the material varies. Neither the gospels nor their details harmonise— not even their liturgical material. We cannot gainsay unsurmountable contrasts and demonstrable shifts in the interpretation of tradition, or diverging theological trends among the evangelists. Contrary to a famous theory, they did not aim to write merely a history of the passion with an extensive introduction. They wanted to write a 'life of Jesus'—certainly, each in his own way. But they did so as messengers of salvation, mingling what was authentic with legendary interpretation. Their interest in facts was overlaid by the task of preaching and by their own particular perspectives.

Mark describes the vanquisher of demonic powers who, in word and deed, brings liberty to the captives, but who has therefore himself to go to the cross and imposes the same necessity on his followers. Christian liberty only exists in the light of Christ crucified, and through those who take up their cross after him. Matthew, with his great discourse and parable complexes, and through the dispute with Judaism, shows Jesus as the End-time Teacher of Righteousness. The Beatitudes part company with mere morality. Men and women are invited into the kingdom of God, and love alone— embracing the enemy too—fulfils the Law. Luke gathers together all the material he can get hold of, arranging it according to time, place and thematic build-up. Forgiveness calls to duty, and duty becomes part of the overcoming of what is earthly, in the steps of the Master. The Church is the present form of the kingdom of God.

John differs from the synoptic gospels, even externally. We see this in Jesus' long monologues; in the inclusion of sensational miracles (probably from a particular source); in the marked divisions in the dispute with the world (represented by the Jews); in the farewell discourses to the disciples; and in the passion, which is glorified as victory over whatever is earthly. It is in correspondence with this that the Gospel has one, single theme: Jesus' glory. He is one with the Father, in whose bosom even the earthly Jesus lies as God's true interpreter. From God he proceeded, and his death, as return to the Father, is the final victory over the world. Everything which men and women need points to him, as does the Old Testament too. In isolation it is misunderstood. Jesus alone is the truth and the life. Whoever passes him by for the sake of any other good remains in sin and death. Even the farewell discourses—which superficially bear on the plight of the believing community after Jesus' death—proclaim present and abiding salvation: the Lord returns to his people as the Paraclete. As the Logos who hears and communicates the Father's voice, he preserves the elect in divine unity and love by allowing them constantly to hear the prophetic Word anew. In this way his kingdom will then also be completed, when all the scattered children of God are gathered into it. The resurrection of the dead has not merely begun with Jesus. It continues wherever light shines into darkness, giving light to those who were blind, and turning enemies into disciples and friends; and whenever there is rebirth in the midst of earthly life.

Style and individuality of thought make one look for the evangelist's congregation outside the main currents of the Church. Atypical themes in the epistles and the sharp dispute in 3 John suggest something like a 'school' on the fringe of the developing mainstream church; while the appendix in John 21 presupposes a conflict with the defenders of the apostolic primacy. Editorial additions seem to aim at adaptation to the traditional views of the Eucharist and the expectation of the End-time. The marked stress on the incarnation in 1 John is probably intended as defence against docetic misunderstandings. Probably there had been criticism of the evangelist's theology, and the circle of his pupils reacted by reducing the areas of attack. But it is especially notable that at the end of the first century there should have been so firm a conviction that all Christians were endowed with the Spirit, and that therefore every individual had a direct relationship to the exalted Lord; remarkable too that the priesthood of all believers is played off against the ordained office. This is resistance against the trend of the time.

But apparently the phase had now begun in which particular dogmatic problems were causing unrest on the remoter horizon, while social differences in the congregations and the advance of the gnostic heresy meant trouble for the young Church. It replied by withdrawing into existing tradition and the postulate of the apostolic succession of a teaching ministry set apart through ordination. The pastoral and catholic epistles offer insight into this process.

Many more details might be given. But it must at least be stressed that the Book of Revelation is the first passionate declaration of the radical breach with the Roman empire. The gospel as a whole has a political dimension. This is nowhere more obviously revolutionary than here. Romans 13 ought not to be discussed without this companion-piece. Here at least, legitimate rebellion by Christians and by the Church is proclaimed, alongside obedience to the powers that be.

The unity of the New Testament remains an open question. We must define what the Gospel of Jesus Christ means before we can identify the centre of the canon and the ecumenical solidarity it implies.

Translated by Margaret Kohl

Jean-Marie Tillard

Theological Pluralism and the Mystery of the Church

ONE OF the most valuable fruits of ecumenism is, it has been said, that it has 'thrown a new light on the difficult problem of the unity and diversity that exists in the Church of Christ'. To this must be added the fact that it has enabled us to discover one of the most fundamental levels of life in the Church. It has in this way given a new emphasis to catholicity.

Throughout history and indeed, if we are to believe what reputable experts in this sphere have said, even in apostolic times,[1] the Christian community has always experienced tension between unity and diversity. Its destiny has always to a great extent depended on the way in which it has borne this tension. Surely a recognition of the difficulty involved in preserving harmony between different interpretations and ways of expressing the one revelation of Christ gives us a key to understanding the schisms that have from time to time shaken the people of God! The universal nature of salvation that is based on keeping to a Word that has been spoken once and for all time and has to be retained in all its purity implies, almost of its own accord, the risk that interpretations will be made that are so diverse as to be regarded as mutually incompatible. Confrontations, misunderstandings and finally ruptures are more often caused by social, cultural and national situations in the places where the Church has become established than by personal ill-will.[2] These are given the rather vague name of 'non-theological factors causing division' in ecumenical texts.

This statement confronts us with quite a difficult problem, since a universality that could be secured at the expense of the entry into the very flesh of humanity would be no more than an abstraction. It would not in any way be Christian. The challenge of the Gospel, which out of resignation is not met by schisms and ruptures of all kinds in the Church, consists precisely in making it possible to achieve a unity of communion (*koinonia*) within which diversity and pluralism are seen as riches and not as dangers.[3]

1. A HISTORICAL SITUATION

One quite clear conclusion can be drawn from an examination of the concrete praxis of the churches throughout the centuries and this is that, even before the great division between East and West and the rupture brought about in the West by the Reformation, that praxis was never the same everywhere. The Church of God has always been pluriform, even during the most striking periods of unity. This has been the case both at the level of praxis and at that of teaching.

(a) This statement cannot be satisfactorily verified simply by citing the obvious differences between liturgical traditions. These have been discussed so much in the past that it would be foolish to reconsider them here. We should rather review the deeper differences in attitude regarding the central aspects of the Christian revelation.

The most obvious case is the evangelical mystery of reconciliation, the seriousness of which was emphasised by the debate about baptism at the time of the crisis brought about by Novatian. Cyprian on the one hand and Stephen, the Bishop of Rome, on the other played a leading part in that debate and it is worth remembering that Cyprian was supported at the synod of 256 A.D. by all the African churches. Clearly, then, it was not simply a personal question of a difference of opinion between him and the bishop of Rome.[4] It was a difference concerning a fundamental question, reflected in the different positions taken by various churches with regard to the Church's penitential discipline and the sins calling for the use of that discipline.[5] Augustine rightly observed that that difference did not lead to a breach in communion.

The debate about Easter also shows how diverse the Church's praxis was and how differently Christians understood their faith. This debate cannot just be reduced to the level of the argument about the date of the feast. It was above all an argument about the significance of Easter. The Syrian, Greek and Latin churches were clearly not in complete agreement about this,[6] the first regarding the Christian Easter primarily as the Pasch or *passio* of Christ as the new paschal lamb and the second as the Pasch or *transitus*, a movement, exodus or going out into the Promised Land. Augustine tried to synthesise the Western view by defining Easter as a movement from this world to the Father through the passion of Christ: 'By his passion, the Lord has passed from death to life and has opened the way for us who believe in his resurrection, so that we too can pass from death to life'.[7] These various interpretations of the same mystery are conditioned by the geographical, historical and cultural situation in which the communities concerned had become established and are not simply the result of theories concerning Easter. They point in fact to a whole range of attitudes, laws and ascetic attitudes, most of which are derived from the environment.

The difficult conflict of the Quartodecimans has often been studied and quoted in this context because it points quite clearly to this cross-influence of place, interpretations of teaching and practical choices on each other. It is well worth remembering what is essential for us today in this case. It is that the Quartodecimans were inhabitants of Asia Minor and historically and geographically close to the Jewish tradition. They celebrated Easter on the same day that Jesus ate the passover meal, following the custom of his people, that is on the fourteenth day of Nisan, 'on whatever day of the week that date occurred'. They ceased fasting on that day. Elsewhere everything was referred back to Sunday. At Rome, about 155 A.D., Anicetus, the Bishop of Rome, and Polycarp, the Bishop of Smyrna, found that they were following different traditions. They did not fall out with each other for that reason, although they knew that their differences were not simply liturgical, but, as Irenaeus pointed out, were also connected with the manner of fasting. In his letter to Pope Victor, who was less tolerant than Anicetus and went too far in his discussions with Polycratus of Ephesus, even threatening excommunication, Irenaeus analysed what was really at stake in the matter. In his opinion, communion in faith should not be endangered by pluralism in praxis and he stressed that 'the difference in fasting confirms agreement in faith'. To support his argument, he called on the evidence of the Church's long praxis. The 'presbyters' who had presided over the church of Rome before Victor's time had not been intolerant of believers whose praxis was different, he insisted, claiming that 'no one should ever be rejected because of that conduct'. Indeed, those presbyters had even sent the Eucharist to them. Anicetus and Polycarp had respected the way in which each of their churches had kept to the customs of their elders. Polycarp's church had, for example, appealed to a Johannine tradition. and Irenaeus had commented: 'As this was the case, one received communion after the other and in the church Anicetus gave the Eucharist to Polycarp, clearly out of defer-ence. They parted from each other in peace. There was peace in the whole Church, whether the fourteenth day was observed or not'.[8]

There was a difference in praxis, then, which was the result of differing social and cultural patterns and this difference was related to a difference in teaching which it encouraged and which in turn encouraged it. This doctrinal difference seems to have been connected with the relationship between the two covenants. The celebration of Easter on the fourteenth day of Nisan and the ending of the fast on that day was tantamount to confessing one's bond with the old covenant, whereas celebrating Easter on the 'first day of the week' was a proclamation of the transcendence of the new covenant. Clearly, then, a theological teaching, which cannot be separated from the context in which it developed, was concealed within the praxis, which was determined by the places that had been so firmly impressed by the 'memory' of the history of Israel. Certain Christians insisted that Jesus was faithful to the praxis of the paschal lamb in the tradition of Judaism, whereas others, including, for example, Hippolytus, tried to show that 'the Lord did not eat the Pasch, but suffered it', in other words, that he refused the passover of the law and became the true Pasch.[9] Traditions inherited from Judaism were obviously influencing and being influenced by later teachings in this case. This is all the more evident in that the different interpretations of the paschal mystery contained within the New Testament itself intervened. But was the Johannine interpretation, according to which the Lord's death coincided with the slaughtering of the paschal lamb because it 'fulfilled' (teleioun) the intention of the latter[10] also not the product of the geographical and historical context in which the communities which gave this particular form to the witness of faith in Jesus were placed? The Johannine tradition with its own interpretation nonetheless remained in communion with the other evangelical traditions because of its faith.

Continuing communion in faith in the Church can go together with great flexibility in the way in which that faith is experienced and interpreted. Considerable differences in attitudes, practices and teachings do not, as Augustine observed, necessarily mean that one is denied the 'right to communion'.[11] It is relevant in this context to recall that, in his De Baptismo, Augustine tried to exonerate Cyprian from all taint of schism and believed that communion of the most true kind could co-exist with the widest possible diversity (as, for example, between Cyprian and Pope Stephen). He admired Cyprian because he refused, during a critical period, to end communion with those who acted differently from himself for reasons to which he was unable to give his approval.

The same attitude can also be discerned in Leo the Great, who allowed a very wide range of traditions, rites and privileges to co-exist in his own local church at a time when there were many immigrants from the East. He regarded the fermentum, the small fragment of bread consecrated by the bishop and mixed on Sunday by each presbyter in his own chalice during the Eucharist, as pointing to the continuation of a 'communion' which transcended all differences because it came from God. According to Bede, writing just over a century later (about 579 A.D.), Gregory, who was Bishop of Rome at the time, believed the same. On this occasion, it was the one Western church that was under consideration. When he was elected to the episcopate, Augustine, the missionary to the Angles, asked Gregory: 'Since faith is one and everywhere the same, how are we to explain the fact that there are differences in praxis in the different churches? Why is there one custom in the church of Rome and another in the church of the Gauls?' Gregory's reply was: 'You know, my brother, the custom in the Roman church in which you grew up. I am glad, however, if, either in the Roman church or in the church of the Gauls or in any other church, you find something which may please the Almighty more and hope that you will remember it and be careful to teach to the church of the Angles, which is new in faith, anything that you may thus acquire from the other churches'. Augustine had the task, then, of using whatever he could find that was pious, honest and religious to build up a kind of body of customs and teachings for the new church of the Angles.[12]

(b) It is clear that Christianity was marked in the first few centuries of the great tradition by an authentic concern to combine unity of faith with diversity of praxis and teaching in accordance with the great variety of situations within which the Gospel was received. The Church was therefore Catholic in the full sense of the word. A form of Church life developed in the East and in the West that was closely in tune with the special way of thinking and acting, the religious tradition and the cultural environment of each. This was, however, not all, since, even within the Eastern and the Western traditions, there was a healthy pluralism.

In the East, for example, there was a different attitude towards asceticism, a different idea of the mystical union, a different liturgy and a different Christology in the churches of Syria, Egypt and Cappadocia. John of Antioch's attitude towards the Nestorian Church was different from that of Cyril of Alexandria, but they ended by rediscovering their communion in faith. Although the traditional distinction made between the school of Alexandria and the school of Antioch should be more subtly defined, there were two different ways of thinking and practising in the Church and these can be attributed to two different historical, cultural and geographical contexts. This tension had also existed in Judaism, between the diaspora and the Holy Land.

In the West, the churches of Rome, Milan, Lyons, Africa, Spain, Ireland and the Angles each had their own way of doing penance, praying and thinking. Irish monasticism bore hardly any resemblance to the kind of monasticism that spread across Europe under the influence of Martin of Tours and Benedict. Different liturgical forms existed even within the same nation—in England, for example, the rites celebrated at Bangor, Salisbury and Lincoln were not exactly the same.[13]

At another level, there have been certain spiritual and religious communities, often with very pronounced characteristics, that have been the result of charismatic inspiration. We have already noted certain expressions of pluralism in the Eastern Church. In all these phenomena, a very important part has always been played by local, cultural, traditional and national elements. A deep sense of faith is made concrete and visible in the material provided by man. Some of those who have played a leading rôle in the liturgical renewal have not been sufficiently conscious of the fact that much more than mere language is involved in this process. Faith has to be interpreted and its content has to be expressed in a way of thinking and acting and this is quite different from simply translating from one language into another.

After the schism between East and West, the latter became gradually more uniform, more and more influenced by Rome and increasingly centralised. A greater diversity was retained in the East. Without overlooking their faults, it is possible to say that the autocephalous churches have allowed individual characteristics to be expressed, while leaving communion in faith not only intact, but also enriched. An important aspect of this can be seen in the emergence of Slav Christianity within the Eastern Orthodox Church, with its very striking impact on the life of the whole Church.[14] There have been frequent points of friction, many of them very painful, but the Orthodox churches have still succeeded in remaining in communion with each other. The recent drama involving relationships with the American church cannot be used as evidence against this fact.

There has been a different development in the West, especially since the Reformation. It is very important to note the part played in this by national and cultural factors. In many cases, doctrinal problems have arisen or have been made worse only in symbiosis with a desire, political in character, to overcome a situation of dependence which is making it impossible to achieve national or local aspirations or to break with an alienating praxis. This would certainly seem to have been the case in England, for example, when there was a doctrinal breach with Rome in the reigns of Edward VI and Elizabeth I following Henry VIII's Act of Supremacy, which had very little theological motivation. Certain aspects of Anglican theology and certain omissions from the Book of Common Prayer can be explained more by the need to maintain a situation than by a doctrinal decision.

I have become more and more convinced in the course of my ecumenical studies that the disruption in the Western church at the time of the Reformation, which had many causes, was to a great extent brought about by clumsiness on the part of Rome. The Roman church failed to achieve a reconciliation between the communion of faith and the diversity that had inevitably come about because of the ways in which the Gospel had become rooted in different societies. It had in fact almost succeeded in imposing a form of civilisation along with the faith and its reaction in the Counter-Reformation (the ultimate fruit of which was to be the influence of the Roman College at Vatican I) and at Trent was also one-sided in that it tended to identify unity too closely with uniformity. This attitude continued to dominate the church's missionary work in the last century, when diversity was regarded as something of marginal, secondary importance in the life of the church. In the West that is described as 'Latin'—although it includes the continents of Africa, Asia and Oceania as a result of missionary expansion in the nineteenth century and these are at the deepest level hardly Latin at all—no diversity was tolerated in the way in which the central aspects of faith was made present and interpreted.[15] Although it was dressed to some extent in local costume, it was the European and indeed the Roman pattern of faith that was exported.

Now, however, we are living in a new period, when the African and Asian churches and the Latin American communities of Christians are insisting that they want to remain in communion with the church of Rome, but are at the same time claiming the right to express their own faith in a praxis that is their own. Vatican II gave great hope, but we see that we are not equipped for the task.[16] There is a feeling about that the wheel is coming full circle and that, with hindsight, the movement towards centralisation (possibly necessary because of a need to make sure of the bases of unity in the Church) was only an interlude. Whatever the case may be, the Church does not seem to know how to let unity and diversity live together. This has, however, given rise to a new pastoral and theological anxiety since there is a desire to listen with pastoral concern for authentic cultural values to the wishes and experiences of Christian communities.

In all honesty, we have to admit that it is not simply the Catholic Church that is confronted with this problem. It is also the case with almost all the missionary churches.[17] It is also worth while adding that several Catholic communities have, since Vatican II, acted as pioneers in the common attempt, to translate faith and make it incarnate. In spite of everything, however, it has to be admitted that the Catholic Church is the least well provided, because it has had less experience than the other churches in recent centuries of healthy pluralism and has to begin at the very beginning. At the level of theology, it has certainly acknowledged sharply opposing positions. In the fundamental Christian teaching about grace, for example, Thomism and Molinism (or the forms derived from it) were completely opposed to each other. But pluralism has hardly entered the structure of the Church and there are signs, such as the periodic interventions into the affairs of the Uniate churches, which show that it is reluctant to accept it, fearing no doubt that communion will suffer if it is accepted.

The situation in the Anglican community is quite different. At the universal level, there are churches within the community with widely differing synodal practices from one country to another and there is at the same time within the whole community a spirit of *comprehensiveness* that is evident in the co-existence of a Catholic and a Protestant or evangelical tradition. There is agreement on the fundamental points, the *regula fidei* and the essential dogmas, since the Church would cease to be Christian without that agreement, but there is tolerance with regard to the rest, in the conviction that differences do not mean an end to communion.[18] There is a wide spectrum of freedom in liturgy, doctrine and pastoral praxis. This comprehensiveness has in practice enabled the Anglican tradition to provide itself with a theology of unity that has made it one of the most valuable agents in the ecumenical movement, the bridging church. It has always had to cling firmly to what is essential within itself, while at the same time giving room to many different views and practices and for this reason it has played a decisive part in the ecumenical movement in stressing the need to look above all for the fundamental points in Christian faith.

(*c*) It is possible to draw at least one conclusion about the nature of theological reflection from this rapid survey that I have made within the limits imposed by this study. It is this: If there is theological pluralism, it is because there is at a more fundamental level a pluralism of cultures, contexts and practical options in the Catholicity of the Church. I have examined several examples of the normal situation in the great Christian tradition and have tried to show that it is not a case of theology being imposed from outside, doing violence to the values of a society by making them conform to a model taken from elsewhere. On the contrary, theology can be seen in that normal situation to be the instrument by which the shared given of the faith is translated—in a way that it has to see is a faithful translation—into the fabric of a community of men and women who are proud of their own characteristics. Moreover, it is not a purely intellectual translation, because it also contains the whole network of attitudes, signs, reactions and intuitions inherent in the *sensus fidelium*.

It is worth stressing in this context that what Blaise Pascal called the 'language of the heart' ('who feels God') is as important here as the language of reason. It cannot, of course, be denied that theology is above all an intellectual activity, but it is only really fulfilling its function if it takes into account the echoes aroused by the Word of God not only in the sphere of reason, but also in the 'cultures of the heart'. There can, after all, be no doubt that there are such cultures formed, for example, by man's desires and secret hopes for 'recognition' and by his suffering and compassion, so well described by Miguel de Unamuno. All these cultures are full of what comes from the soil in a mysterious complicity with nature, enough for poetry and song—often a sad song—to emerge from it. It is above all in them that the Gospel takes flesh and is made one body with the density of the human body. It is from them that this incarnation derives all its truth. It is these cultures that have made it impossible for Francis of Assisi to have existed outside Umbria, Dietrich Bonhoeffer to have lived and worked apart from the tragedy of Hitler's Germany, Martin Luther King to have functioned outside the black American ghetto or for Oscar Romero to have been an archbishop in any church other than the one in El Salvador. If theologians do not try to include these 'cultures of the heart' among their materials, their theology will not be totally in touch with its object. It is very important for them to gather into their theology what, in the power of the spirit, the African, the Peruvian peasant, the Indian woman, the oppressed labourer and the sinner (whether he is rich or poor) who is imprisoned within his wrong attitude, 'feels' in his heart or her heart about the Gospel.

Although he gave it in a very different context, it is worth recalling Gregory the Great's advice to Augustine of Canterbury here, when the latter was troubled about differences in praxis in different churches. Discursive reasoning will put this level of the *sensus fidelium* in touch and dialogue with what it can discover about the objective sense or meaning of Scripture, about the sense or meaning that has been proclaimed unceasingly at all times and in all places in the great Christian tradition with the aid of those who are committed to carrying out the task of the Church's *magisterium*, and about the homogeneous nature of revelation. It will distil a coherent and articulate expression from the common faith, whilst taking into account the authenticity of its translation, in communion with the faith of every community of believers, into the soul of this particular people or this group of human beings.

It may be thought that a process of this kind might put the communion of faith severely to the test. Might it not happen, it may be objected, that the co-existence of so many different translations would raise pluralism to such a high status that the particular would gradually come to be regarded as more important than the universal in the Church? And as soon as unity ceases to exist at the deepest level, true Catholicity also ceases to exist and then all is lost! It can hardly be right to correct one excess (that of uniformity) by creating another (that of fragmentation). Are we over the barrel?

Let us reconsider in this case the wisdom of the great Tradition. Theologians and those whose task it is to excuse the *magisterium* (at all levels) have to work *together* and not in opposition to one another to make sure that there is at the same time a unity of faith and a diversity of translations and that the tension between unity and Catholicity does not deteriorate into conflict. This is surely a typical case of the complementary nature of ministries within the people of God. Chalcedon provides an excellent example of this in that it protected the freedom and right to exist of the theology of Antioch by integrating the thrust of it and in this way justifying it in the face of a crushing attack. Instead of condemning or rejecting it, it upheld it as a possible option, at least in those aspects of it that did not call into question the divine dimension of the mystery of Christ.[19] Various scholars have pointed out[20] that the definition of 451A.D. is based on the conviction that there is a deep consensus of faith underlying the diversity of the two rival theologies. The Council of Chalcedon did not reject one or other of these theologies, but rather provided a broader base which would guarantee the orthodoxy of the definition, thereby allowing it to be expressed within the framework of Catholicity. In this way, the Council was acting in a truly 'Catholic' manner.

2. ROOTED IN THE ACT OF FAITH

Theological pluralism, then, exists throughout the whole spectrum of the Church's Catholicity and we must therefore also expect it to be rooted in the act of faith and to have an inner coherence with the essence of faith. This is something that derives from the definition of all theology as *fides quaerens intellectum*.

(*a*) Believing is, in the biblical sense of the word, freely receiving the God who revealed himself in Jesus Christ. There is only one welcome or reception, but it contains two positive affirmations, two 'yeses'. They are intertwined, although they are also quite distinct from each other. One 'yes' is incarnate in the other, which it transcends.

The first of these affirmations can be described as our positive reception of God's proposition (his Gospel or good news), which forms the essence of the kerygma. We say 'yes' to God's plan (Eph. 1:11) as proclaimed by the first witnesses of the risen Lord. We agree to being saved. This is what Peter advised those who heard him to do (Acts 2:40). Once we have received God's love, we can at once derive benefit from what he has brought about in Jesus Christ for mankind. We can enter the one, indivisible Body of Christ, in which all divisions have been overcome in his blood—he has broken down the wall that separates us, hatred (see Eph. 2:14).

Even in the kerygma of the apostles, there is already evidence of pluralism. The different evangelical proclamations contained in the New Testament do not all place the mystery of salvation offered by God within the same perspective. One theologian has expressed this very well, saying that there is 'one Jesus, many Christs'.[21] Those who proclaimed the message in the early Church were not in agreement about who should hear the good news. At Pentecost, Peter proclaimed it as the fulfilment of a promise made to the holy people, whereas Paul treated it at Athens as a response to the quest of religious men. Both, however, wanted to encourage their listeners to reply 'yes', less in the sense of keeping to a doctrine *about* God than in the sense of accepting an approach made by God.

Seen as an acceptance of salvation, this 'yes' has basically the same intention and object in the case of all who are moved by the Gospel sufficiently to accept what it has to offer. It therefore forms the basis of unity in faith and of communion as instituted by God himself. *Because of God*, unity and diversity are not in this case in conflict with each other.

(*b*) At baptism, then, the believer says 'yes', but this does not mean that he does so for the primary and formal purpose of knowing anything *about* God. Because he is human, however, he is bound to inquire who that God is who has offered him salvation and what that act implies. If it is not open to an eventual understanding of the significance of the act, his baptismal 'yes' will verge on the absurd and easily be mistaken for a purely voluntaristic way of acting or an enthusiastic response of an illuministic kind. Man is created in God's image and he has an instinctive urge to know. He is therefore always trying to discover the meaning of that to which he has given his consent and to know something about God and his salvation, to define the nature of what was accomplished in Jesus Christ, to understand the bonds uniting Christ with his Father and to explore the content of salvation. This quest for meaning is a guarantee that his 'yes' to the kerygma is serious. It is worth noting in this context that Peter made an explicit connection at Pentecost between accepting God's offer of salvation and what the people knew about the God of the covenant and that Paul at Athens took care to base what he said on man's rational search for God.

This 'yes' *to* God therefore becomes a 'yes' *about* God, but, whereas the first 'yes' comes primarily from the heart, the second comes from the intelligence illuminated by the Spirit of God. It is therefore essentially noetic and its formal object is not a proposition made by God, but rather propositions about God, in other words, theology, dogma, definitions of faith or simply doctrinal tradition.

The Christian community plays an essential part in the process of working out the material content of this noetic 'yes'.[22] This is so much the case that everything we have spelled out about the function of cultures, contexts, historical and geographical setting, attitudes and practices can be verified at this level. This explains why, when all the evidence in the New Testament points to the one person of Jesus of Nazareth (the one who was baptised in the Jordan by John the Baptist and who went about doing good), who died, was raised from the dead and exalted on the right hand of the Father, very many different things were said about that one man by the first apostolic communities. It is clear that the noetic interpretation of the Johannine communities is not precisely the same as that of the communities whose 'tradition' was handed down by Matthew. These differences persist, however, despite the fact that all the early Christian communities were convinced that the Jesus they had known was the same as Christ the Lord proclaimed in the kerygmas. There is, then, a difference contained within the 'yes' spoken by the members of those communities to the statements or teachings *about* God, Christ or salvation. That difference is, nevertheless, contained within their 'yes' *to* God and to the proposition made *by* God, with which they were all in unanimous agreement and which forms the basis for their communion at the deepest level. From the apostolic age onwards, then, we may conclude, faith was 'Catholic'. It was Catholic in the full sense of the word because of the influence on each other of this 'yes' to the offer *from* God and the 'yes' to a search for knowledge and understanding—which varied according to

F

the tradition in question—of what was revealed *about* God and implied in his salvation.

As soon as the early Christian communities had been constituted, their members were 'evangelised' by them. When they were baptised, those first believers were necessarily integrated into one or other of those communities. It is obvious that they kept to the Gospel as proclaimed by the community to which they belonged and the Gospel was inevitably proclaimed in a way that was marked by the noetic or doctrinal tradition of the community in question; this it did receive, but passed on, sometimes superimposing its own impression on it. Christians, then, only said 'yes' to God in baptism, the 'yes' that enabled them to be grafted on to the one Body of Christ, via a 'yes' bearing on the view of a certain community and a certain tradition. That 'yes', which was said to what the community in question professed *about* God and his plan, was the instrument of the 'yes' said *to* God and creating communion.

Each baptised Christian thus became, as far as his faith was concerned, the recipient of the interpretation of the shared faith that was provided by his community and of that community's way of understanding the one event of Jesus Christ. But as faith had to be lived in praxis, each Christian consequently also lived according to that interpretation. If he was baptised at Antioch, he would share the same faith as his fellow-Christians in Alexandria or Milan and he would also proclaim the same essential truths, as affirmed solemnly in the Church's creeds and the definitions promulgated by the ecumenical councils, that is, those councils which included the churches of every tradition. Those creeds and conciliar definitions would draw his attention to the central axes from which he should not depart because they point to the 'way of salvation'. He would also lead the same evangelical way of life of the covenant of grace. But he would do all this in a different way from his brethren baptised in other communities. The all-embracing 'yes' of his faith would, along with the 'yes' that he said to the proposition made *by* God, inseparably integrate a 'yes' to what quite soon came to be regarded as the doctrinal tradition of his community, in other words, a 'yes' to the community's position *with regard to* God.

(*c*) The whole issue of Catholicity as we conceive it is concentrated in this datum. Unity and Catholicity are ultimately based on the mystery of faith. The problem of the Church as one and at the same time Catholic in the sense in which it has been used here has always existed at the level of the act of faith and in the incarnation of our 'yes' *to* God (made above all in our heart) in a more noetic 'yes' concerned with teaching *about* God, Christ and salvation.

If it crosses a certain threshold, the pluralism of traditions in doctrine can degenerate into fragmentation or even schism, since it is always possible for one interpretation to produce a wrong assessment of an essential teaching or to accuse other interpretations of doing this. If there is doctrinal pluralism, great care has to be taken to preserve on all sides those elements which, if they were lost, would cause communion to be lost. If unity in faith is not to be served at the expense of doctrinal diversity, then the latter has to rely on a praxis of unity. It is possible that this problem arose even in the Johannine communities, in that some regarded others as less orthodox and probably even as in error.[23] It is therefore quite possible that Chapter 17 of the fourth gospel represents an attempt to save the *koinonia* either from a uniformity which would sterilise the germination of true Catholicity or from an explosion which would destroy unity. That was, as we have seen, the real concern of the Council of Chalcedon.

The problem is still with us today. I am either Catholic or 'Orthodox', according to the way in which my community thinks of the connection between the Spirit and the Son in its doctrinal tradition. I am either Anglican or Catholic, according to the way in which it thinks of the Eucharist. The essential question is whether this doctrinal pluralism constitutes a breach in communion in faith. A diversity of doctrinal traditions and a battery of technical terms may even conceal a profound agreement with regard to what has to be explained. We have therefore to go beyond formulae. There is in this instance the well-known example of Basil the Great, who, when he was pressed, was able to use the technical terminology of a theological tradition, but who normally preferred to keep to the language of Scripture in his expression of shared faith, because he was afraid of being an 'obstacle to those who are in the way of salvation because of the severity of (his) propositions'.[24] It is necessary to make the rock that we all share appear through the details.

(d) Two important points arise by way of theological reflection from what I have said. The first has to do with the part played by what I have called noetic or doctrinal interpretation in the dynamism of clinging to faith within a given community. For theological reflection is without any doubt one of the most important factors in the slow process by which a tradition comes into being in the Church.

In connection with theological and doctrinal pluralism, I have spoken of how the Gospel is normally rooted in a culture or a social context and have insisted that this is what makes the presentation of faith acceptable to that particular culture or society, because faith is in this way in harmony with that society's spirit, memory, past experience and expectations. The Gospel simply cannot be proclaimed in the same way in Jerusalem and in Athens, to a United Nations assembly, as Pope Paul VI did, and to a gathering of poor peasants in Brazil. (Theological or doctrinal) pluralism is therefore connected not only with the culture in which faith is embedded, but also with its presentation and with what is able to bring it to birth through the whole world. This is to signify its importance. Theological research is as valuable an instrument in the process of evangelisation as the visible incarnation of the life of the Church itself. It plays an important part in conditioning the 'yes' that is said, via a doctrinal reading of a datum of faith that is directly linked to real aspirations, to a proposition made by God. Far from being a 'luxurious form of knowledge' (sic) which we can easily do without, it is a most important element in the Church's mission. If theology is carrying out its task properly, moreover, the proclamation of the Gospel will not be overshadowed by an empty form of apologetics that does a disservice to faith.

The second point, which is often overlooked, but is equally important, is that theological pluralism is only authentic in so far as it is based on a praxis of communion and unity. If this praxis of communion exists, there should be no divisive barriers created by an absence of mutual knowledge and understanding and each tradition will have an intuition of the limits beyond which it should not go if it is to remain faithful to the truth of faith. This is especially applicable when attempts are being made to explore as fully as possible the ways in which faith is made incarnate in the social context. As soon as other groups fail to recognise their own faith in the way in which it is lived and proclaimed by another group, then the danger is already present that there may be a breach with the shared faith that is based on the revealed Word of God. Theologians, then, have to remain closely in touch with the Church's *magisterium* on the one hand and the *sensus fidelium* on the other and in this way critically assess the tradition of their own community in the light of the faith and praxis of other Christian communities. This is particularly important in those communities in which a tradition is beginning to develop, as in the case of Africa and Latin America. It is essential to preserve communion and critical assessment is only possible and credible if Christians live in *cor unum et anima una* in their different groups and communities. It is on that that the objectivity of the assessment depends.

At the same time, however, attention must be paid to the rights of communion. If this does not occur, there is always a grave risk that nationalism or the need for self-assertion will take precedence over the content of faith and even entirely eclipse it in the theology or tradition of a given community or society. There is sufficient historical evidence to show that this fear is not groundless. A local theology that is indifferent to communion

F*

may well lead a community of baptised persons in the direction of a political system rather than to the God and Father of Jesus Christ.

All that I have been able to do in this article is to make a few soundings and to discuss a few intuitions. I have not been able to examine them very deeply, but they may help the reader to recognise how important the question of theological pluralism is today in the Church of God.

Translated by David Smith

Notes

1. See, for example, Raymond E. Brown *The Community of the Beloved Disciple* (New York 1979); James D. Dunn *Unity and Diversity in the New Testament* (London 1979).

2. See S. L. Greenslade *Schism in the Early Church* (London 1953) especially pp. 55-73.

3. See Y. Congar *Diversités et communion* (Paris 1982).

4. See the *Sententiae episcoporum numero LXXXIII*, ed. Hartel *CSEL* 3/1 pp. 435-461.

5. For the first Christian centuries, see H. Karpp *La Pénitence, textes et commentaires des origines de l'ordre pénitentiel de l'Eglise ancienne* (Neuchâtel 1970).

6. This has been pointed out by R. Cantalamessa *La Pasqua nella Chiese antica* (Turin 1978).

7. *Enarr. in Ps.* 120, 6; *CC* 40, 1791.

8. Eusebius *Hist. Eccl.* V, 24, pp. 1-18.

9. Hippolytus *PG* 92, 81. The first group goes beyond the Syrian churches. The Johannine tradition and the synoptic traditions play a part here. The problem is quite deeply rooted.

10. It is much more than simply a question of the calendar, at least according to Mlle Annie Jaubert.

11. *De Bapt.* III, 3, 5.

12. See Philip McShane *La Romanitas et le Pape Léon le Grand* (Tournai 1979) p. 306.

13. Bede *Hist. Eccl.* 27.

14. See N. Zernov *Three Russian Prophets, Khomyakov, Dostoievsky and Soloviev* (New York 1944); A. Gratieux *Le Mouvement slavophile à la veille de la Révolution* (Paris 1953); *id. A. S. Khomiakov et le mouvement slavophile* (Paris 1959).

15. One is reminded of the attempts to latinise the Maronite churches, which were in any case strongly attached to the Roman see.

16. I have selected the following titles from a long list because I have found them particularly valuable: A. Hastings *Christian Marriage in Africa* (London 1973); L. V. Thomas and R. Luneau *La Terre africaine et ses religions* (Paris 1975); Vincent Mulago *Simbolismo religioso africano* (BAC 1979); in collaboration, *Libération ou adaptation ? La théologie africaine s'interroge* (Paris 1979); J. M. Ela *Le Cri de l'homme africain. Questions aus chrétiens at aux églises d'Afrique* (Paris 1980); A. Shorter *Théologie africaine, adaptation ou incarnation ?* (Paris 1980); J. M. Ela, R. Luneau and C. Ngendakuriyo *Voici le temps des héritiers, églises d'Afrique et voies nouvelles* (Paris 1981); A. Scarin *Chiesa locale, incarnazione e missione. Il principio di incarnazione nella evangelizzazione secondo il pensiero dell'episcopato africano* (Bologna 1981); E. Uzukwu 'Christian Liturgical Rites and African Rites' *Bulletin de théologie africaine* 4 (1982) pp. 87-110; *Religion and Society. The First Twenty-five Years* (1953-1978) ed. Richard W. Taylor (Madras 1982).

17. What is the difference between an Anglican form of the Eucharist at Lincoln and in Bangalore?

18. For 'comprehensiveness', see S. W. Sykes *The Integrity of Anglicanism* (London 1978) pp. 8-15, 128-131; Stephen Neill *Anglicanism* (London 1977); Emmanuel Amand de Mendieta *Anglican Vision* (London 1971).

19. Henry Chadwick's Preface to André-Jean Festugière *Actes du Concile de Chalcédoine, Sessions III-VI (Le Définition de la Foi)* (Geneva 1983) pp. 3-12, especially pp. 6-12, in which the author demonstrates this well in his analysis of the definition.

20. *Ibid.*, p. 12.

21. James D. Dunn, the work cited in note 1, p. 216.

22. I use the word 'noetic' here in the wider sense of the 'fruit of mature reflection' and it therefore includes an approach leading to everything that constitutes the doctrinal spectrum of the life of faith, that is theology, dogma and definitions of faith.

23. See Raymond E. Brown, the work cited in note 1.

24. See Emmanual Lanne 'Le Comportement de Saint Basile et ses exigences pour le rétablissement de la communion' *Nicolaus* 5 (1982) pp. 303-313.

Nicholas Lash

Theologies at the Service of a Common Tradition

1. INTRODUCTION

ALL HUMAN utterances occur in a context. And the contexts in which they occur modify their meaning. Having been invited to reflect on the ways in which an irreducible theological pluralism might contribute to the sustaining, recovering and deepening of unity in faith, it may therefore be useful to indicate certain features of the context in which this essay was written.

The general context is that of a non-denominational Faculty of Theology in a secular university. Most of my colleagues, and most of our students, are Christians. The teachers in the Faculty, all of whom have been appointed for their competence in a particular theological discipline, with no thought given to their denominational allegiance, represent, as it happens, eight different denominations: we include Baptists and Lutherans, Anglicans and Catholics, Methodists and Presbyterians.

In such a context, a number of things soon become apparent. In the first place, the diversity of experience that we bring to our work enriches the 'catholicity' of our conversation.

In the second place, working in a secular university in which no church body has any say in the appointments that we make, our ecclesial responsibilities are less immediately apparent than they would be if we taught in a 'Catholic' or 'Protestant' Faculty. Most of my colleagues are, in fact, very conscious of their ecclesial responsibilities. But we serve less as 'spokesmen' for particular traditions than as 'mediating interpreters' of a common tradition.

In the third place, in so far as we discover (as we often do) that we share a common faith, this discovery occurs not in spite of but because of the diversity of language and experience, memory and thought-form, that we bring to our work. We discover that diversity, far from being necessarily a barrier to common conviction, can be a significant condition of the depth and quality of such conviction.

In the fourth place, however, we also often discover how fragile is our unity, how profound our divisions in faith. But, almost invariably, these divisions are not drawn along denominational lines. They lie deeper than the divisions that appeared in the sixteenth or eighteenth centuries; divisions that are now in process of being healed. They are rooted in fundamental perceptions of the relationships between theology and culture, Christian faith and human striving, the eschatological reign of God and particular patterns of human ordering in culture and politics.

This brings me to a second, more specific context in which this paper was produced. As I write, in March 1983, the pope has just completed a visit to Central America. If there is one lesson for European theologians to learn from the struggles and the suffering of that part of the world, it is surely that questions concerning the relationships between unity in faith and theological diversity are embedded in intractable practical problems of culture and politics, power and economics, suffering and the quest for human dignity and fraternity.

Theology has a part to play, perhaps even an indispensable part, in the clarification and resolution of such problems. But any theologian who loses sight of the *modesty* of his contribution, who supposes that clarification of the theological issues can of itself be a major factor in determining the course of events, has fallen victim to the kind of idealist academic *hubris* from which Christianity in modern times has already suffered quite sufficiently.

It was with considerations such as these in mind that I decided to situate the specific issues to which I had been asked to address myself in a broad context of problems of human and Christian unity. The result, inevitably, is that instead of providing the carefully detailed examination which these specific issues undoubtedly demand, all I can offer is an impressionistic sketch of the wider agenda or framework within which such detailed examination should proceed.

2. INADEQUATE MODELS

(a) 'Classicism'

'On classicist assumptions there is just one culture. That one culture is not attained by the simple faithful, the people, the natives, the barbarians. None the less, career is always open to talent. One enters upon such a career by diligent study of the ancient Latin and Greek authors. One pursues such a career by learning Scholastic philosophy and theology. One aims at high office by becoming proficient in canon law. One succeeds by winning the approbation and favour of the right personages. Within this set-up the unity of faith is a matter of everyone subscribing to the correct formulae.'[1]

The classicist can tolerate diversity of expression, for catechetical or apologetic purposes. What he cannot tolerate, or even understand, is the suggestion that a genuine and irreducible diversity of methods and arguments, of discourses that are not mutually translatable one into another 'without remainder', can be other than a threat to common faith.

The 'classical', normative, concept of culture has been superseded by an 'empirical' notion according to which 'A culture is a set of meanings and values informing a common way of life, and there are as many cultures as there are distinct sets of such meanings and values'.[2] On this account, unity of faith will find expression in a common way of life, not in common subscription to some single set of formulae.

However, to say that classicist notions of culture have been superseded is not to say that they have ceased to exist, but only that the assumptions on which they rest have been historically, sociologically and philosophically undermined. Not everyone recognises the occurrence of this shift, and hence classicist assumptions survive like beached whales on the shores of contemporary culture. Even beached whales, however, are a force to be reckoned with. No small part of the pain and misunderstanding in contemporary theological debate arises from the fact that we have to deal not simply with the bewildering diversity of contemporary theology, but with the survival (by no means *only* in 'Rome') of the classicist mentality for which the very fact of significant theological diversity is *prima facie* evidence of error and discord, and a threat to common faith.

On non-classicist assumptions, no individual, no group, no institution, stands *outside* that complex and frequently conflictual process of remembrance, interpretation, discrimination, hope and inquiry, within which meanings and values are sought, affirmed and sustained. It does not follow that there are no standards, no criteria of truth and value, but simply that *arbitration*—the reaching of decisions in matters of meaning, truth and value—is a permanent task and process in which a structured community is unceasingly engaged. Such arbitration is not, and cannot any longer be, 'gnostically' conceived as the exclusive prerogative of a group of 'authorities' or 'experts', uniquely 'in the know' and situated outside the process which requires such arbitration.[3]

(b) 'Liberalism'

For the majority of those theologians who work in the universities of the Western world, 'unity of faith' is certainly not a matter of 'everyone subscribing to the correct formulae'. On the contrary, such subscription is suspect. Pluralism is encouraged and diversity fostered. The strength of the 'liberal' tradition derives from its recognition that disagreement and diversity are evidence of the irreducible complexity of patterns of human experience, and hence of the partial and limited nature of all knowledge and understanding.

On liberal assumptions, the life of the Church (as of the wider society) is thought to resemble as unending academic seminar. But those who take part in the seminar, frequently unmindful of the social and economic privilege which makes their performance possible, tend to overlook the extent to which theoretical disagreement is but the abstract expression, in the order of ideas, of conflicts which, outside the seminar room or the 'salon', frequently find harsher and more concrete form. In other words, the weakness of theological, as of political, liberalism lies in its neglect of the calculus of power and in the inadequacy of its analysis of the grounds and sources of conflict and contradiction.

A common tradition, a common way of life, is not sustained by discussion alone. It requires the structuring of common experience, and the pursuit of agreed goals and purposes in common action. Any movement or way of life which is to sustain its identity and vitality, *as* a movement, has to be able to decide and to declare what it stands for. And if a movement or way of life is concerned with meanings and values that are central to human need and human flourishing, then, in the measure that it calls in question the operations and the legitimacy of the 'powers that be', it can expect to meet not merely with 'disagreement' but with more practically enacted forms of resistance.

Neither the 'classicist' nor the 'liberal' model can furnish us with a convincing account of the ways in which a theology acknowledged to be irreducibly pluralist in character can contribute to building up and sustaining the unity of Christian faith. 'Classicism' cannot accommodate genuine diversity, and 'liberalism' construes that diversity in too abstract or 'idealist' a manner. In search of an alternative account, therefore, we must begin by looking further afield.

3. THE UNITY OF MANKIND

The problem of 'unity of faith' is part of the problem of the unity of the Church and this, in turn, is part of the problem of the unity of mankind. It is with this broader notion, with questions concerning the content, scope and criteria of the concept of a 'common human nature', that we must begin.

The unity of mankind may be a biological fact: that is for the scientists to say. But, even if it is a biological fact, even if we appropriately describe some animals (and only those) as 'human' in virtue of their belonging to a single biological species, that fact only provides us with a small part of what is meant by sharing a 'common human nature'. Whatever be the case where other species are concerned, in our case, 'genetic fraternity' is not enough to warrant the claim that we share a common nature. The reason for this is that we are curious animals which do not only breed and feed, and make social arrangements (many other animals do as much). We also speak and consider, tell stories, construct policies and make plans. Our cultures, the meanings and values that inform our ways of life, form *part* of our nature. In other words, for all members of the species to share a common *human* nature, they would have to share a common life, a common hope and a common language: that is to say, a common tradition. And this, in significant measure, they fail to do. It follows that there is an ethical and political as well as a biological component to the concept of 'human nature'. The 'unity of mankind', far from being a mere biological datum, remains a permanent task and responsibility.

Moreover, on a Christian account of these matters, human beings have not only a common origin, as creatures of God made in his image; they have also a common destiny, in virtue of the promise of God who is confessed to be not only Creator but Redeemer of the world. The concept of a 'common human nature', of the 'unity of mankind', has, therefore, not only biological, ethical and political components, but also an eschatological component. The redemption of the human race would be the imperishable constitution, for all members of the species—dead, living and as yet unborn—of that common humanity which, in so many ways, we manifestly lack. The unity of mankind is, at one and the same time, a fact, a task, and the object of our hope.

4. THE CHURCH AND THE UNITY OF MANKIND

The Church, according to Vatican II, is called to be the 'sacrament of intimate union with God, and of the unity of all mankind'.[4] But the Church does not realise its vocation simply by *declaring* that this is its nature and destiny. It has unceasingly to seek to become, in fact, that which it purports to be.

The practical and political implications of the Church's vocation to sacramentality will be different in different circumstances. There is no single set of such implications which can be timelessly, ahistorically inferred from the doctrine of *Lumen Gentium*.[5] Nevertheless, there are some very general or formal considerations which are worth bearing in mind. The most important of these concern what we might call the 'positive' and 'negative' aspects of the Church's sacramental vocation and responsibility. The positive aspect arises from the fact that it is the vocation of the Church to be the sacrament, in this world, of God's kingdom. The negative aspect arises from the fact that God's kingdom is not to be *identified* with any past, present or future state of affairs in this world. Let us consider each of these aspects in turn.

Sacraments, like all symbols, must be 'legible'. An illegible symbol, like an unintelligible language, is a contradiction in terms. If only Christians are able to 'read' the Church as symbolising the unity of all mankind, then the Church is not yet the adequate symbol of that unity. The Church, in any particular place and time, has at its disposal an inherited symbolic vocabulary: artistic and architectural, musical and poetic, narrative and theoretical. By drawing on the resources of this vocabulary, Christians seek to show what it is that faith declares to be mankind's origin, task and destiny.

In so far as what Christians *do* contradicts what, in the language they construct from their symbol-stock, they declare themselves to be about, they declare the 'legibility' (and hence the sacramentality) of the Church is threatened. But, for all its importance and urgency, my primary concern in this paper is not with this ethical dimension of the problem of sacramentality.

Even when deeds and words, action and discourse, closely correspond, it may still be the case that the symbols used are (by and large) expressive only of the history and experience of some one class or interest-group, some one race, culture, sex or nation. In this case also, a Church which drew upon so restricted a range of resources could only be an impoverished symbol, an attenuated and 'one-sided' sacramental expression, of the unity of all mankind in the mystery of God.

In the world as it is and has ever been, there is no such thing as 'universal' memory or 'universal' language. There are only particular memories and particular languages. Therefore, in speaking only 'from' some particular circumstances, places and times, the Church does not succeed in speaking intelligibly or accessibly *to* those whose circumstance and experience, language and memory, are 'other' than those that it has made its own. And a Church which employs a 'language' or symbol-stock that is, in fact, not appropriable as its own by other than a portion of the human race (whether that portion be Indo-European or masculine, rural or industralised, rich or poor) can only be an impoverished sacrament of the unity of *all* mankind.

(It should hardly need emphasising that what is at issue here is not whether the message of the Gospel, as 'encoded' in particular languages and symbol-systems, is universally 'agreeable', but whether or not it is universally accessible. We have to ask, of each particular human group, in each particular set of circumstances: what is the message that can actually be 'heard' *from here*, when Christians speak and act in whatever ways they do, in fact, act and speak?)

From the very beginning, from Peter's vision at Joppa and the Council of Jerusalem,[6] Christianity has acknowledged *in principle* its vocation to catholicity. But the shift from 'classicist' to contemporary concepts of culture carries with it a qualitative shift in our perception of the implications of that vocation. 'Catholic' is what the Church is under obligation to seek to become, and the quest for catholicity is frustrated by the exclusion from its symbol-stock, whether by accident or by design, of any of the irreducibly diverse languages that constitute the memory and interpret the experience of mankind. This is the positive aspect of the Church's vocation: its responsibility to become, in fact, the sacrament in this world, throughout this varied world, of God's kingdom.

The negative dimension arises from the fact that the unity which we seek, that 'common human nature' whose realisation will be the fullness of the kingdom of God's grace, is not attainable within the confines of historical process. There is no past, present or future state of affairs in this world that could be declared *identical* with the kingdom of God. The vocation to catholicity therefore carries with it the responsibility prophetically to resist all absolutisation of historical particulars: of particular persons, circumstances, languages, images and institutions. The God who acts, appears and speaks in history remains the hidden God, the God who may never be identified with particular forms of his appearances.[7] Totalitarianism, whether from the 'right' or from the 'left', whether secular or ecclesiastical, whether of language or of organisation, is always idolatrous.

In circumstances in which some such idolatry prevails or threatens, the sacramental expression of eschatological hope for the unity of *all* mankind must take the negative form of resistance on behalf of those whose particular experience and identity is being obliterated and suppressed, forgotten and excised from the definition, narrative and memory of mankind.

5. UNITY OF FAITH AND UNITY OF THE CHURCH

(a) Aspects of Unity

Having commented briefly on the concept of the 'unity of mankind', and on the Church's responsibility unceasingly to seek to become that which it is called and constituted by God's grace to be: namely, the sacrament of human unity in the mystery of God, we now turn to the problem of what might be meant by 'unity of faith'. (Thus, at each stage of the inquiry, we are narrowing the area of concern.)

Here, the first thing that needs to be said is that the Christian confession that there is but *one* Lord and *one* faith, far from being an expression of sectarian arrogance or ethnocentric imperialism ('we are right and the rest of the world is wrong'), is a confession of trust in the singleness or consistency of God's grace. A Christian doctrine of God, a doctrine of God's grace as man's salvation, seeks to tell the tale of *all* human experience, *all* human striving, not only as the story of man's irreducibly diverse approaches to God but also, and more fundamentally, as the story of the diverse expressions of God's consistent approach to man. Central to the Christian perception of the mystery of God is the conviction that the story of all nature and all history is, ultimately, the story of a *single* process of divine self-bestowal, a single 'economy' of creation and salvation. The unity of saving faith is the unity of God's single constitutive and transformative self-gift.

How is the unity of God's gift to appear, to find expression, in the diversity of human experience, perception and response? We distinguish, traditionally, three aspects of that single gift; the aspects named as the 'theological' virtues of faith, hope and charity.

Where charity, or love, is concerned, the unity of God's gift finds expression, or fails to do so, in reconciliation and the making of peace. Not the illusory peace that comes from exhaustion, fear, or the imposition of order, but the peace that the world cannot give and which, within the history of sin, and striving, and suffering, it never unsurpassably attains: there is an incompleteness in the peace 'made through his blood, on the Cross', so long as blood continues to be shed.

God's gift is already and always one in the singleness, the consistency, of divine action. Man's self-constituting[8] acceptance of that gift is her permanent task and responsibility, the achievement of which is eschatological. Because unity in love, the peace of Christ, is God's gift, therefore failure in love, the rupture of relationship between individuals and between groups, may never simply be *accepted* (though it may have to be *endured*), with resignation, as insuperable tragic fact, as the end of the matter. Thus to accept the finality of failure would be to despair.[9] Because the unsurpassable achievement of unity in love is eschatological therefore, within history, all talk of 'complete' or 'full' unity is dangerously misleading.

Everything that we have said about unity in love as God's gift, man's task and responsibility, and as the object of eschatological hope, can also be said of unity in faith (except that, in the kingdom, faith becomes unclouded vision, whereas love, purified, endures). Unity in faith, like unity in love, admits of infinite gradations: it waxes and wanes, is stronger or weaker and may, from time to time, be ruptured and broken. Within history, all talk of 'complete' or 'full' unity in faith is dangerously misleading.

This symmetry between unity in faith and unity in love is obscured from view by the influence of the classicist assumption that 'unity of faith is a matter of everyone subscribing to the correct formulae'. Once abandon classicist assumptions, however, and the problem of how unity in faith might be discerned, sustained, sought and recovered, demands altogether different descriptions.

Before outlining such a description, there is one further point to be made, for the sake of completeness. I have said nothing about 'unity in hope'. What is the relationship between common hope, common faith and common love? I suggest that unity in hope, sharing a common hope, *mediates* between unity in faith and unity in love. Thus, on the one hand, sharing a common hope helps those who share a common faith, a common conviction, to grow together in love, common life and responsibility. Conversely, sharing a common hope helps those who share a common life and responsibility to grow together in common conviction. Where unity in hope is absent, the quest for solidarity, for unity in life and love, degenerates into activism and pragmatism, and the quest for common faith degenerates into an intellectualist quest for formulas of concord.

(b) Mutual Recognition

I remarked earlier that, on non-classicist assumptions, unity of faith will find expression in a common way of life, not in common subscription to a single set of formulae. But, since it is a common way of *human* life that is in question, it certainly does not follow that 'words do not matter'. Unity of *confession* of faith, the unity of the Creed, is integral to unity of faith, because common life that cannot find expression in common language is less than human unity. Agreement, which means agreement that finds expression in *language*, is a necessary though not a sufficient condition of the unity of any human movement or way of life.

But, if such agreement does not necessarily consist in subscription to a single set of formulae, in what might it consist, and what are the criteria of its achievement? We can approach these questions by observing, firstly, that the paradigm or 'focal' forms of Christian (as of Jewish) religious discourse are narrative in character. More specifically, they are 'autobiographical' both in the sense that they are 'self-involving' (which will be shown in their performance, or use, and not necessarily in their grammatical form) and in the sense that, as self-involving, they situate the speaker (or the group for which he is a spokesman) in a particular cultural, historical tradition: 'My father was a wandering Aramean'. The Christian is the teller of a tale, the narrator of a story which he tells as *his* story, as a story in which he acknowledges himself to be a participant. The Christian creeds are abbreviated statements of a story which, as the autobiography of the narrators and of the Christ 'in whom' they seek to tell their story, is a *particular* story and which yet, as the story of the origin, course and destiny of the world, purports to express what is *universally* the case.

Abandon the unity of the Creed, and its universal import is threatened or implicitly denied. Evacuate it of its particularity, and it ceases to be capable of truly expressing any particular history.

In a culture that is, or is presumed to be, more or less homogeneous, the tension between these two aspects of the function of the Creed may not become apparent. But, once the irreducible diversity of culture and memory, history and experience, language and thought-form, is taken seriously then, as Karl Rahner has remarked, 'There will no longer be any one single and universal basic formula of the Christian faith applicable to the whole Church'.[10]

In these circumstances, the unity of the Creed, no longer maintained by subscription to a single formula, will be maintained by continual quest for *mutual recognition*.[11] The stories that differently express different experiences will not be verbally identical. But, if each creed, each 'abbreviated statement' of faith, containing what are taken to be the essential elements of the Christian narrative, is to be a *Christian* creed, a 'catholic' and 'orthodox' creed, and not a narcissistic celebration of nationalist, sectarian or particularist egotism and self-interest, then it must be offered as, and be capable of being accepted by others as, a different version of the same story, not a different story.

The temptation is to suppose that such mutual recognition can only occur if there is, somewhere, some neutral 'standard of measurement' by which the adequacy of particular creeds could be assessed. But, on non-classicist assumptions, there is not, nor could there be, any such standard. Not even the Scriptures can fulfil this function, because it is precisely the adequacy of each creed as a 'reading' of the Scriptures, through particular experience, which is in question.

However difficult it may be, from a theoretical point of view, to reconcile the unity of the creed with the diversity of its 'versions', to differentiate between different stories and different versions of the same story, a simple analogy may indicate how such mutual recognition could occur in practice. I am a native English speaker who is reasonably fluent in French. It is not at all far-fetched to imagine that, in conversation with a native French speaker who was reasonably fluent in English, we might find ourselves not only understanding each other but reaching *agreement*, while yet acknowledging that what it was that we were agreed about could not be put in quite the same way in each of our two languages.

It is important to notice that, in such situations, maintained linguistic diversity is *necessary* in order for agreement to occur and to find expression (unless, of course, one of us brought pressure to bear to force the other to abandon his native tongue); it is by no means evidence of imperfection or incompleteness in the agreement arrived at. Moreover, the process of 'dialogue' which issued in the agreement would, if conscientiously undertaken, purify the self-understanding, and render more precise the language, of each of the participants. With the introduction of this analogy, however, I have begun to touch on questions concerning the tasks of theology in contributing to, sustaining and deepening unity in faith.

6. THE TASKS OF THEOLOGY

The relationship between theology and the practice of faith has taken, we might say, three primary forms in the history of Christianity.

Until the seventeenth century theology was, first and foremost, 'faithful inquiry': *fides quaerens intellectum*. In these circumstances, so long as unity in faith was sustained in social practice—in a relatively homogeneous culture drawing upon a common stock of symbols—theological diversity and disagreement (often acute) posed no direct threat to unity in faith. (It was when the unity in culture or social practice was eroded that theologies—Eastern and Western, for example—became mutually unintelligible.)

From the late seventeenth century,[12] as the Church became 'citadel' rather than 'sacrament', the tasks of theology shifted from inquiry to *defence*, demonstration and 'proof'. The theologian became a propangandist for Church doctrines, and theological pluralism was perceived as a threat to the foundations of the single, well-ordered citadel.

From the early nineteenth century (in Protestant theology) and the mid-twentieth century (in Catholic theology), as the Church began to recover a sense of its sacramentality, the task of theology increasingly became that of *mediating* between the practice of faith and the irreducibly diverse languages and social practices—in work, art, narrative and organisation—in which human self-understanding finds primary expression.[13]

In these circumstances, a multiplicity of theologies becomes a necessary, but not sufficient, condition of the achievement, recovery and deepening of unity in faith. Today, it is no small part of the theologian's task, as 'mediating interpreter', to help different groups of Christians to attain and sustain that agreement, that 'mutual recognition', in which unity in faith is realised and strengthened.

To that general account, there are four comments to be added. In the first place, theologians must exercise their responsibilities, as mediating interpreters, not only between our diverse human 'presents', but also between the present and the past. They must be 'recoverers of memory', using the resources of historical scholarship to criticise the selective stereotypes by which we shape the past to suit our present preferences.

In the second place, it is not the theologian's business, as mediating interpreter, to foster agreement 'at any price'. The divisions, the painful conflicts, that exist between Christians (as between all other human beings) are not healed or reconciled by 'papering over the cracks'. Nevertheless, the theologian, as mediating interpreter, as the servant of unity, will seek *critically* to reflect on the ideological distortions of his *own* group, class, national or cultural consciousness.

In the third place, there is not, nor can there be, any grand synthesis, any 'global theology'. Pseudo-universalist theologies often, in their excessive abstractness and generality of expression, serve unity in faith less well than those which seek accurately to reflect cultural particularities depicted in narrative and poetry. (It is no accident that the Psalms, the Gospel narratives and, come to that, the plays of Shakespeare, are more 'universally accessible' than any abstract conceptual system.)

In the fourth place, the emphasis on the irreducible diversity of culture and context, memory and experience, must not encourage the illusion that different contexts and cultures are, in principle, mutually 'impermeable' or illegible. Not only are there constants of human experience—of suffering and joy, labour and hope—however diverse their specific form and expression; but the 'shrinking of the planet'—economically and politically, through travel and the mass media—offers opportunities as well as threats to the sustaining of a common tradition, a common service of sacramentality.

Finally, what are the conditions that must be fulfilled in order for any particular theology to assist the Church in its quest for catholicity? We might mention two. In the first place, each theology must genuinely *be* a 'particular' theology, expressive of some particular context and circumstance, seeking to mediate between that context and some other particular 'place' or places of experience, meaning and value. This necessary specificity of the contexts of dialogue affords another reason for individual theologians, or 'schools' of theology, to be exceedingly modest in their ambitions.

In the second place, theological modesty has a further aspect inasmuch as the theologian, the facilitator of mutual recognition, works *at the service* of the Church's quest for catholicity. It is not the theologian's business to tell other people what to believe or how to believe it, but simply to facilitate that growth in mutual understanding which may enable him and his brethren, 'near' or 'far off', to discover, sustain, and deepen, common life, common work, common conviction and a common hope. The many theologies exist at the service of a common tradition.

All human utterances occur in a context. And the contexts in which they occur modify their meaning.

Notes

1. B. J. F. Lonergan *Method in Theology* (London 1972) pp. 326-7.

2. *Ibid.*, p. 301.

3. See N. L. A. Lash *Voices of Authority* (London 1976) pp. 84-100.

4. Vatican II *Dogmatic Constitution on the Church (Lumen Gentium)*, para. 1.

5. See N. L. A. Lash *A Matter of Hope. A Theologian's Reflections on the Thought of Karl Marx* (London 1981) pp. 237, 252.

6. See Acts of the Apostles, chh. 11, 15.

7. Anyone who supposes that the Incarnation of the Word constitutes an exception to this rule has overlooked distinctions drawn with great care by the Councils of the early Church.

8. See R. Panikkar 'Faith, a Constitutive Dimension of Man' *Journal of Ecumenical Studies* 8 (1971) pp. 223-254.

9. Even 'in the shadow of the bomb', these things are more easily said in a climate of relative economic prosperity and political stability than they might be elsewhere. Nevertheless, whatever one's situation, to refrain from saying them would be to refrain from acknowledging one's *own* need for forgiveness.

10. K. Rahner 'Reflections on the Problems Involved in Devising a Short Formula of the Faith' *Theological Investigations* XI, (London 1974) p. 230. On the general issue, see Rahner 'Pluralism in Theology and the Unity of the Creed in the Church' *Investigations* XI, pp. 3-23; 'The Foundation of the Belief Today' *Investigations* XVI (London 1979) pp. 3-23.

11. See N. L. A. Lash 'Credal Affirmation as a Criterion of Church Membership' *Church Membership and Intercommunion*, ed. J. Kent and R. Murray (London 1973) pp. 51-73.

12. See. B. J. F. Lonergan 'Theology in its New Context' *A Second Collection* (London 1974) pp. 55-67.

13. See K. Rahner 'Philosophy and Philosophising in Theology' *Theological Investigations* IX (London 1972) pp. 46-63.

Bulletin

Enrique Dussel

Theologies of the 'Periphery' and the 'Centre': Encounter or Confrontation?

THE 'ECUMENICAL Association of Third World Theologians' (EATWOT) has just come to the end of its first stage (1974-1983). This is a good point at which to begin a discussion of its significance.

1. ANTECEDENTS

In October 1974 I talked to François Houtart about the possibility of organising a dialogue between theologians of the peripheral countries of Asia, Africa and Latin America.[1] On 6th January 1975 he wrote to me: 'I have made contact with an African theologian, and one from Asia, to discuss the project'.[2] Together with Stan Lourdusami (India) and K. Bimwenyi we drafted the first Circular, which was sent out in April of that year to ten theologians on each continent. In this circular it was said for Africa:

'The bishops of Africa and Madagascar consider that a certain kind of theology of adaptation is completely out of date. They prefer a theology of incarnation. . . . The young churches of Africa must encourage by all means research into an African theology!'[3]

From Asia we published the declaration from Cardinal J. Paracattil of India:

'It is imperative that a new orientation is given to evangelical work . . . Theology should reformulate its theses in intelligible native idioms and indigenous philosophical terms.'[4]

From Latin America we quoted from a text of the II General Conference:

'It is impossible to try to impose fixed universal moulds . . . We must treat with particular importance the study and investigation of our Latin American reality in its religious, social, anthropological and sociological aspect.'[5]

The response of the theologians we contacted was enthusiastic and unanimous. 'The time has come for a meeting of the theologians spread over the periphery.'[6] We needed to create a discourse, a dialogue, an 'alliance'—in its spiritual and political sense—between the militant theologians of the periphery—*directly* between them—*without being divided* by the presence, problems, interests—from the folkloric to the anthropological or out of 'good will'—of the theologians of the 'centre' (called the First World). It was practically an impossible project, because how would it be possible to bring about such a meeting without financial help from the 'centre' and still maintain total freedom with regard to possible conditions attached? It had to be a *direct dialogue without going through the centre.*

After the renewal begun by the II Vatican Council (1962) and the Assembly of the WCC in Delhi (1961) things changed a great deal in the early years of the Seventies.[7] A new start was made in Asia, beginning in 1949 in Bangkok, when the Protestant churches began to reflect on the social revolution[8] and continuing with the Tokyo Ecumenical Conference of Asia (July 1969), the First Pan-Asian Conference of Bishops in November 1970, the VI Assembly of the CCA and the All-Asia Theological Consultation in 1977 in Manila.[9] In their consultation in New Delhi in February 1970, the bishops had declared: 'above all we have proposed to establish the Church of the poor more authentically'.[10] In the Synod Cardinal Paracattil exclaimed: 'The Catholic church is neither Latin nor Greek nor Slave, but universal. Unless the Church can show herself Indian in India and Chinese in China, and Japanese in Japan, she will never reveal her authentically Catholic character.'[11]

In *Africa* renewal began in far-off 1956 with the publication of *Des Prêtres noirs s'intérrogent.*[12] Then there was the All Africa Conference of Churches in 1969 in Ibadan, under the leadership of Burgess Carr.[13] The Symposium of Episcopal Conferences of Africa from 28th to 31st July 1969 declared that 'the present urgent problem is the struggle for the development of countries, and peace. The Church cannot ignore poverty, hunger, sickness, ignorance, attacks on freedom, without betraying its mission.' In the Thrid AACC Assembly from 12th-24th May 1974, there was still discussion of John Gatu's *Moratorium*[14], and the position of the bishops in the Roman Synod of 1974 was its expression.[15]

In *Latin America* after Sucre (XIV Assembly of CELAM in 1972) there began the persecution of liberation theology[16] and of Christians who try to make a more scientific analysis of reality. A long time has passed now since the works of J. Comblin (*Fracaso de la Accion Catolica*, 1957), Juan Luis Segundo (*Situacion de la Iglesia en el Rio de la Plata*, 1959), the meetings at Rio or Montevideo at which Gustavo was present in 1964 or the Paris meeting 'Latin America and Christian conscience'.[17] Liberation theology, which appeared explicitly in 1968, looked like being suffocated under the weight of militarism (coups in Brazil in 1964 but which took effect in 1968; in Bolivia in 1971, Chile 1973 etc.). This meant it was necessary to form a 'front' and join forces. In 1975 together with Enrique Ruiz Maldonado, we organised the Mexico Meeting, to evaluate the theological work of the continent.[18] 'Dark night' covered Latin America and it was necessary for us to make contact with our brothers and sisters in Africa and Asia.

After the Nairobi World Council of Churches Conference in 1975, Sergio Torres, who had been organising theology in the Americas, became the director of what was later called EATWOT.

2. THE FIVE MEETINGS OF THEOLOGIANS FROM PERIPHERAL COUNTRIES

The First Meeting took place from the 5th to 12th August 1976 in Dar-es-Salaam (Tanzania);[19] we were twenty-two theologians from Asia, Africa, Latin America and minorities from central countries. The intercontinental dialogue was begun. The Second Meeting took place in Accra (Ghana) from the 17th to 23rd December 1977.[20] This meeting was particularly dedicated to Africa. One hundred and two of us attended, as some theologians from other continents had also been invited. We studied trends in African theologies, from the class-based and antiracialist theology in South Africa, to the most culturalist, in its affirmation of national identity, in other regions. At the Third Meeting (Sri Lanka), which took place from the 7th to 20th January 1979,[21] dedicated to Asia, attended by over eighty, the Asian theologians showed a balanced openness to the economico-political and religio-cultural problems of a minority Christianity amid gigantic poverty. The Fourth Meeting in Sao Paulo (Brazil) from the 20th February to 2nd March 1980[22] dealt with the theme of Base Communities; 104 members from 42 countries attended. Lastly, from 17th to 29th August 1981 we met in New Delhi,[23] there were 50 of us from 27 countries and we stated that 'after five years of theological investigation, we are meeting to evaluate our work, to list criteria and resources and so find a new direction for our future work'.[24]

3. FUNDAMENTAL AGREEMENT: INTERNATIONAL STRUCTURAL SIN: 'VERTICAL' DOMINATION

The most unanimous agreement between the theologians from the periphery of world capitalism, dependent and dominated by productive and fiscal capital in its stage of transnationalisation was:

'The analysis of the situation of Third World countries . . . revealed a general agreement that *poverty* and *oppression* are the most obvious characteristics of the Third World. Massive poverty is increasing . . . But this poverty is not an accidental fact. It is the result of *structures of exploitation and domination*; it derives from centuries of *colonial domination* and it is reinforced by the present international *economic system*.[25]

This means that there exists an international 'structural sin', a domination by the centre countries through very advanced science and technology as an essential part of the organic composition of capital.[26] This analysis is a *determining factor* in all the theological reflection of the peripheral countries. Sin has a name (capitalist exploitation: 'world capital').[27] This theology is clear. It is not reformist, social democratic, simply liberal—in its North American or European sense.

This 'vertical' domination is reflected in the peripheral country by another kind of 'vertical' domination:

'The people are also dominated by a local élite in the Third World, so that the masses are doubly exploited: at national, and at international level'.[28]

This avoids the populist ambiguity of declaring that foreign powers are guilty of all evil and the national oligarchies or bourgeoisie innocent. The same thing happens with culture, a 'vertical' domination of one culture by another:

'*Culture*' is the basis of a people's creativity and way of life. It expresses their vision of the world, ideas about the meaning and destiny of human life, ideas about God'.[29] 'Western domination has also damaged native *religious* cultures. The change in the means of production has had a negative effect on the social models and *religious* values which have sustained our communities for centuries'.[30] 'Vertical' domination of culture over culture (from the centre or on the part of a dominant class) or of one religion over another, and hence the 'missionary' spirit as an offensive crusade against other religions needing to be vanquished.[31]

G

TYPES OF 'VERTICAL' DOMINATION

country from centre	dominant class	oppressive culture	hegemonic religion
↓	↓	↓	↓
periphery	dominated class	oppressed culture	repressed religion

4. OTHER KINDS OF DOMINATION OR SIN ('HORIZONTAL')

As well as these kinds of economic, political and ideological domination, there is the domination of one sex over another, one ethnic group over another, one race over another etc.

> '*Women* all over the world and at all levels suffer enormously from the models of masculine domination in social and cultural organisation'.[32] '*Racialism* is an evil present in many societies in the world, expressing itself in various kinds of dehumanisation and segregation'.[33]
> 'In India the *caste* system is a powerful and oppressive institution'.[34] 'We recognise the existence of ethnic minorities in every country . . .'[35]

Thus the forms of sin are many and deep, always structural, historical, unnoticed. These 'horizontal' forms of domination are determined by the 'vertical' but also determine them in their turn. Thus the problem of women or the Black race is different at the centre and at the periphery, in dominant or working class. But sexist patriarchy and racialism also determine the relationship between the periphery and the centre and the domination of one class over another. The one determines the other, although not in the same way.

TYPES OF 'HORIZONTAL' DOMINATION:	masculine sex	→	feminine sex
	white race	→	black race
	caste 1	→	caste 2
	ethnic group 1	→	ethnic group 2

5. MOBILISATION OF THE OPPRESSED OR LIBERATION

All the theologians noted an increasing pressure for liberation by the dominated—at all levels:

> 'The growing awareness of the tragic reality of the Third World has caused an irruption by the exploited *classes* and humiliated *races* . . . The Third World is beginning to speak with its own voice, demanding justice and equality'.[36] 'This irruption expresses itself in revolutionary struggles, political uprisings and liberation movements. It is the rising of *religious* and *ethnic* groups seeking to affirm their own identity, of *women* demanding recognition, of the young protesting against the system of dominant values'.[37]

The *negative* situation of oppression is confronted by positive action, which seeks 'alternatives' or the 'discernment of utopias':

> 'In the face of this dark picture of the capitalist world, socialism seems to offer the only alternative. However the socialist countries, both in the Second and the Third World have problems to solve . . . The struggle for political and civil rights, the demand for greater participation'.[38]

A theology of work (in which possession of the product would be for the satisfaction of needs and not an instrument of power), a clarification of the contradictions of 'real' forms of socialism were topics frequently discussed.[39] There was agreement on the general strategy: 'We reject capitalism which has been responsible for most of the internal and external evils of our societies'.[40] But the overcoming of capitalism in the periphery must ensure 'economic development together with *respect for religions, cultures and human freedom*'.[41]

6. THE THEOLOGY OF THE CENTRE HAS NO RELEVANCE FOR THE PERIPHERY

The theologies of the periphery have a new paradigm, a new articulation of theological *theory* with the *action* of the oppressed. The hegemonic theologies in Europe and the US still minimise the irruption of these theologies (and place them in the end chapters of their 'systematic theologies': social ethnics, theology of culture . . . i.e. folklore, fashion, superficialities).

Nevertheless the judgment upon them is clear:

'Traditional (existing) theology (of the centre) . . . has not found reasons for opposing the evils of racialism, sexism, capitalism, colonialism and neocolonialism . . . The instruments and categories of traditional theology (of the centre) are inadequate for contextual theology. It is also closely connected to Western culture and to the captialist system . . . It has remained highly academic, speculative and individualist and ignores the social and structural aspects of sin'.[42]

It is frequently a *theology of domination* because it has identified itself through its model of *Christendom* (which is not Christianity, as Kierkegaard reminded us) with the dominant countries, classes, races, sexes.[43] This is the crisis for the dream of a theology claiming *universality*, which was only the *particularity* of the centre which was and still is able to impose itself on others through the power of its economy, technology – even at the level of libraries, publications, theological administrative structures. On the other hand some theologians from the centre 'are responding to the questions raised by their situation as centre of world capitalism and as the place where various oppressed minorities live'.[44] It is therefore necessary to work out an 'international theological division of labour' in which theologians humbly assume their partial, continental, local tasks. They must at the same time be aware of factors determining their situation.

7. NEW PARADIGM. THEOLOGY ARTICULATED OUT OF MILITANCY AND ACTION

There was general agreement on the type of articulation of theory and practice in theology:

'Theology is not a mere academic exercise'.[45] Interpretations of life based on the faith of people at the base, expressed in their cultural modes as liturgy, devotions, stories, drama, song, poetry, constitute genuine theology. In its formal sense, as a science, theology is a discipline requiring academic and technical competence. But the *two forms* of theology are relevant only if they derive from involvement with the oppressed and a liberating awareness'.[46]

Theory or theology is a second act that emerges from practice, from involvement, militancy, organic connection with the oppressed as persons, sex, race, ethnic group, class, nation. It is a theology of the oppressed or theology of liberation of the poor countries:

> 'The starting point for Third World theologies is the struggle of the poor and oppressed against all forms of injustice and domination. The sharing by Christians in these struggles offers a new *theological locus* for reflection'.[47]

Both standpoint and audience in mind are new. That is to say, the subject of a theological discourse articulates himself in relation to the pre-eminent subject of theology: the oppressed:

> 'In order to be truly liberating this theology . . . is articulated and expressed to the oppressed community, using the technical skills of biblical scholars, sociologists, psychologists, anthropologists and others . . . All theology is conditioned by the situation and class awareness of the theologian'.[48]

All theology, including that of the periphery, has an 'ideological' status: It arises, takes shape and serves particular *doings*. It is a relative 'knowing' (not absolute) of a 'doing': 'Father, forgive them because they *know* not what they *do*' (Luke 23:34). It is a true 'epistemological break',[49] since theology is not 'ours'.[50] Either it explicitly serves the oppressed or it is, at least implicitly, a theology of domination. This requires a new systematisation of theology, a new universal history of the Church and its dogmas, a new biblical theology (and their respective dictionaries), new exegesis, new pastoral theology, new ethics . . . It transforms fundamental theology but also the theology of creation and the Trinity, Christology and ecclesiology . . . the whole of theology.

Furthermore, it is a post-ecumenical theology. Now we are *already united*, because the causes of divisions existed and exist only in the centre:

> 'The different Christian communities, Catholic and Protestant share the same historical and eschatological project . . . If it is true that the poor preach the Gospel to us, it is also true that they open the way towards our unity'.[51]

In our theology of the peripheral countries there is no division between work from originally different communities. Our problems exclude the questions which divide the Christians of the centre.

8. MEETINGS BETWEEN THEOLOGIES FROM THE PERIPHERY AND THE CENTRE

We have already indicated a necessary distinction between theology of liberation (of the oppressed, who may be from the centre as in 'Black theology') and the theology of the peripheral countries (which may not be a theology of liberation, as with the excellent ethnotheology of John Mbiti).[52] There have been many meetings between theologians from the centre and those from the periphery. Let us recall *a few*.

There were three kinds of 'meetings' between theologians from the centre and the periphery, before the Sixth Geneva Meeting in 1983. The first kind were meetings which I shall call '*partial*'; secondly 'global mainly from the *capitalist* world'; thirdly 'global mainly from the *socialist* world'. As one of the first kind (Accra 1973) the Black Theology of the US held meetings with African theologians,[53] and progressive Spanish theologians set up a dialogue with Latin American liberation theologians (Escorial 1972).[54]

In 1973, in Accra the aim was to build bridges, but the difficulty arose from the fact that in this case the theology from the centre was a liberation theology (the 'Black Theology' of the US). In El Escorial in 1972 the reception given by the more than 400

European participants was enthusiastic, because the theological 'new winds' helped them in the anti-Franco struggle in which they were engaged. The meetings under the title Theology in the Americas (Detroit 1975 and 1981)[55] were more in the nature of an agreement on the part of theologians of the American continent (central and peripheral).

The first *global* meeting, but mainly from the capitalist world, between the most eminent centre theologians from Europe (liberals, progressive and conservative) and theologians from the periphery (Edward Bodipo-Malumba from Africa, Paulo Freire and Hugo Assmann from Latin America) and liberation theologian from a minority of the centre (James Cone) took place in May 1973 in Geneva.[56] The meeting was 'three days of challenge, confrontation, anger, frustration and resignation', said Mernie Mellblom.[57]

In 1977 we organised with Jorge Pixley, in Mexico from 8th to 10th October, a meeting between theologians from the US and Europe and Latin American liberation theologians and Sergio Arce, a Cuban.[58] This meeting served as a preparation for the Matanzas Meeting (Cuba) from 25th February to 2nd March 1979, on 'Gospel and Politics', at which there were 70 theologians from the developed socialist countries (USSR, Poland, Czechoslovakia, Yugoslavia), underdeveloped (Angola, etc.), capitalist countries from the centre (Europe and US) and Latin American countries dependent upon capitalism. It was a meeting which completely changed the perspective and we were able to glimpse the possibility of a global North-South, East-West dialogue in theology. In the *Final Document* we see clearly the 'vertical' domination (economic, political ideological) of imperialism over the dependent countries ('Today the Gospel is preached from the periphery')[59] and 'horizontal' domination (sexist, racialist, etc.) ('Gospel, racialism, sexism').[60] This meeting was the most comprehensive and complete to date, but the African and Asian presence was limited.

At the Sixth EATWOT Meeting in Geneva, from 5th to 13th January 1983, attended by 81 participants, the new element was the important presence of feminist theologies, which were both militant and expressed in academic language. These theologies took their place side by side with theologies of racial, cultural, religious and class oppression. The almost complete exclusion of professional European theologians—decided by the European groups who summoned the theologians from the centre—gave the dialogue a particular configuration: what might have been a more technical theological encounter became a dialogue of militant theologies, which lacked experience of dialogue in terms of the centre and had almost no experience at all of dialogue with the periphery. This was why it was difficult to define clearly the difference caused by the fact that a particular feminist, anti-racialist, or class theology arose from the centre or the periphery. Sometimes, for example, the feminist theologies, expressed their thesis homogenously, without distinguishing what type of dialogue was taking place between feminist theology of the centre and the periphery. It was a militant meeting of theologies of liberation, with many ambiguities. The centre-periphery division (with the sole exception of Julio Santana's talk on the world economic crisis) did not function as a means of dialogue between the centre and the periphery. It was a beginning and as such extremely useful. It showed the patience needed in this kind of process which takes many years.

9. ACHIEVEMENTS. MEETING OR CONFRONTATION?

The theologians of the periphery do not reject the theologies of the centre but they are beginning to set a distance from them:

'The theologies of Europe and North America are dominant in our churches. They represent a form of cultural domination. They must be seen as responses to *particular* situations in these countries. Therefore they must not be adopted *uncritically* or without our asking if they are relevant in the context of our countries'.[61]

It is not a question of rejection, but of taking and using these theologies from a *different* theological situation. This implies a certain *negation* to begin with (our theology is *not* the theology of the centre). After that it requires a slow, hesitant, creative beginning which still has not produced mature results, starting with the first realisation that takes the form of confrontation (Geneva 1973?). Then a slow journey to build a *new analogical theology*. The elaborate theologies of Europe or North America can ignore this new theology or declare that it is unscientific. But just as history gave us the 'modernist crisis' and since then nobody can help thinking historically, so liberation theology presents us with objective conditions and in future nobody will be able to avoid thinking in terms of conditioning by class, country, sex, race, etc. This will not just be one chapter in the history of theology, but it will require a *complete* and *total re-reading of the whole of theology*.

In the dialogues between the peripheral countries, differences arose between Africa, Asia and Latin America, and also the differences between the centre and the periphery. We also saw possible solutions to enable us in the first place to understand the other's position and then to draw up methods and categories (a paradigm) appropriate to a future *world* theology, a new analogical totality, which will be constructed in the Twenty First century after particularities have been noted and spelt out (including the *particularities* of Europe and the US).

Translated by Dinah Livingstone

Notes

1. See EATWOT *The Emergent Gospel* (Orbis Books, New York 1976) pp. 1-2; O. K. Bimwenyi 'A l'origine de l'Association oecumenique de théologiens du Tiers Monde' *Bulletin de théologie africaine* II, 3 (1980) pp. 41-53.

2. Correspondence from the Association's archives.

3. See *Documentation catholique* 1664, 17th November (1974) p. 995. Declaration by bishops in the Roman Synod of 1974.

4. Separated by 4 pages, on p. 3 entitled 'Indigenisation and Evangelisation', Roman Synod, Sermon of 30th September 1974, extracted from *Ernakulam Missam* Nov. (1974).

5. *Final Document*, Medellin 1968.

6. See some replies published by Bimwenyi, in the article cited in note 1 pp. 42-6.

7. See the development of this decade in my works *A History of the Church in Latin America. Colonialism to Liberation* (Grand Rapids, Michigan 1981) pp. 125ff; *De Medellin a Puebla* (Sao Paulo 1982-3) vol. I-III; and Aylward Shorter *African Christian Theology* (Orbis, New York 1977); Gerald Andersen *Asian Voices in Christian Theology* (Orbis, New York 1976) pp. 6ff. The economic crisis of 1973-4 produced a general crisis in the periphery, increased the foreign debt in 1974 to 45 thousand millions (30% more than in 1973). On 5th May 1976 Henry Kissinger declared in the IV UNCTAD in Nairobi: 'The United States is more able than any other country to survive a period of economic war. We are in a position to ignore unrealistic proposals'—from the peripheral countries (*Excelsior* (Mexico) 8th May (1976) p. 10). See Samuel Silva Gotay *El pensamiento cristiano revolucionario en America latina* (Sigueme, Salamanca 1982) pp. 29-72.

8. See EATWOT *Asia's struggle for full humanity* (Orbis, New York 1980) (III Wennappuwa Meeting, Sri Lanka) pp. 4ff. We should also think of the Prapat meetings of 1957, the East Asian Christian Conference of 1958; the East Asian Christian Conference meeting of 1965, and in particular Emerito Nacpil's proposal on the 'critical Asian principle' (see 'The Critical Asian Principle' in Douglas J. Elwood *What Asian Christians are thinking* (Quezon City, New Day P 1976) pp. 3-6.

9. See Preman Niles 'Toward a framework of doing theology in Asia' in *Asian Theological Reflections on Suffering and Hope* (Singapore, CCA 1977).

10. 'Eglise et développement' in *Nos evêques parlent*, no. 6, Justice and Peace Committee (Rome 1971) p. 9.

11. Bede Griffiths *The Christian Ashram*, p 54.

12. *Presence africaine* (Paris 1956). See T. Tshibangu 'The Task of African Theologian' in EATWOT *African theology en route* (Orbis, New York 1979) pp. 73-9; and *ibid.*, pp. 23-35. A meeting took place in Rome in connection with the Second Vatican Council (see *Personnalité africaine et catholicisme* (Paris 1963) and the Kinshasa Faculty of Theology organised meetings on African theology in 1959 up till 1967. These are published by CERA (*Cahiers de Religions Africaines*).

13. See *Pour une theologie africaine* (Clé, Yaundé 1969).

14. See *Bulletin of the All-African Conferences of Churches* 7 (1974) nos. 1-3.

15. See. P. A. Kalilombe 'Self Reliance of the African Church' in *II* pp. 46ff.

16. See the works quoted in note 7 above.

17. See *Esprit* (July 1965) which published the 'Latin American Week' which we organised at that time: 'Chrétientés latino-americaines' (pp. 2-20).

18. See *Liberacion y cautiverio*, Meeting Issue (Mexico, 1976). The Second Latin American Meeting became a dialogue between social scientists and theologians in August 1978 in San José (Costa Rica). The Third Meeting was organised for July 1983. There have been many other informal meetings in New York, for Puebla, in Petropolis, etc. Many Latin American liberation theologians took part and they had a continental character.

19. EATWOT *The Emergent Gospel* (*EG*) quoted in note 1.

20. *Idem, African Theology en route* (*AT*) quoted in note 12.

21. *Idem, Asia's Struggle for Full Humanity* (*AS*) quoted in note 8.

22. *Idem, The Challenge of Basic Christian Communities* (*BC*) (Orbis, New York 1981).

23. The English edition is due from Orbis Books, New York in 1983 (*ND*).

24. *Documento Final* N. 5. (*Teologia desde el Tercer Mundo. Documentos finales*, DEI, San José 1982, p. 77.)

25. ND. N. 9-10 (p. 78). See my article 'Analysis of the Final Document of Puebla: The Relationship between Economics and Christian Ethics' in *Concilium* 140 (1980) pp. 101ff. See other final declarations: *EG*, N. 6-8 (pp. 260-3); *AT*, N. 9 (p. 190); *AS*, N. 5 (pp. 152-3); *BC*, N. 6 12-13 (pp. 232-4).

26. 'Technology is an essential element in our development and it is controlled by the rich countries, increasing our dependence' (*ND*, N. 12 p. 78).

27. *Ibid.*, N. 11, p. 78.

28. *Ibid.*, see *EG*, N. 12 (p. 264); *AT*. N. 14 (p. 191); *AS*. N. 13-14 (p. 154); *BC* N. 12ff (pp. 232 ff).

29. *EG*, N. 53 (p. 91).

30. *Ibid.*, N. 20 (p. 80); *EG*, N. 8.h (pp. 262-3); *AT*, N. 21 (p. 192); *AS* N. 8 32 (pp. 153 and 157); *BC*, N. 7, 14 (pp. 232-3).

31. 'We note that the old missionary strategies have lost their validity . . . The missionary Church . . . used education as a means of domestication' (*AT*, N. 17, 18 (p. 191). See *EG*, N. 19-21 (pp. 265-6); *AS*, N. 25 (p. 156); *BC*, N. 45 (pp. 238-9).

32. *ND*, N. 17 (p. 79). Cf *EG*, N. 8, g and 36 (p. 262; *AS*, N. 21 (p. 155), *BC*, N. 16, p. 234; see N. 45 and 87, and pp. 239 and 245.

33. *ND*, N. 16 (p. 79); *EG*, N. 8, G and 36 (pp. 262 and 271); very especially *AT*, N. 10-12 (pp. 190-1); *BC*, N. 7 and 16 (pp. 232 and 234). Cornel West links (as in the New Delhi Declaration: 'Class oppression is closely related to discrimination based on race, colour, sex and cast': N. 14, p. 79) the question of racialism with class when he writes: 'Racial status contributes greatly to Black oppression. But middle class Black people are essentially well-paid white or blue collar workers (in US) who have little control over their lives primarily because of their class position, not their racial status . . . Therefore class position contributes more than racial status to the basic form of powerlessness in America' (*Prophesy deliverance* (Westminster, Philadelphia 1982) p. 115).

34. *ND*, N. 15 (p. 79).

35. *AS*, N. 22 (p. 155); *BC*, N. 10 (p. 233). The 'ethnic group' is neither caste nor race. It is more like a 'nation' or historical community, a social formation.

36. *ND*, N. 26-7 (pp. 82-3).

37. *Ibid.*, 'Struggles for liberation throughout history are not isolated or accidental events. They are part of a dialectical process. They are a reaction to overwhelming oppression' (*Ibid.*, N. 28). See *BC*, N. 7-11 and 19-26 (pp. 232-5).

38. *ND*, N. 24 (p. 81).

39. See *EG*, N. 9-11 (p. 263): 'Socialism also has problems to solve especially in the safeguarding of human freedom and the real cost in lives of the revolutionary process' (*ibid.*). This does not mean either opting for reformism or for the 'third way'. 'We believe that the basic insight of socialism is closer to the Gospel teaching than the postulates of capitalism. Nevertheless we maintain a critical attitude towards the mistakes made by certain historical experiments in socialism. . . . Socialism must face these weaknesses and this requires serious analysis and evaluation' (*ND*, N. 30, p. 84).

40. *ND*, N. 31, p. 84.

41. *Ibid.*

42. *Ibid.*, N. 32-33 (p. 85).

43. See *EG*, N. 15-25 (pp. 264-7). What in New Delhi was called 'traditional' theology must be understood, in Dar-es-Salaam, as both 'conservative' and 'liberal' theology. There is no reference to the 'neoconservatism' of the centre, which is the theology most opposed to that of the peripheral countries.

44. *ND*, N. 37, p. 86. 'Some European theologians are talking about "European theology" in order to distinguish it from the old theological idea of "universal theology" ' (*ibid.*). Theology is becoming 'analogical' (see my article 'Historical and philosophical presuppositions for Latin American Theology' in *Frontiers of Theology in Latin America* (Orbis, New York 1979) pp. 185-212).

45. *ND*, N. 40, p. 87. 'We reject, as of little significance, an academic type of theology, separated from action' (*EG*, N. 31, p. 269). See *AT*, N. 21-3, pp. 192-4; *AS*, N. 26-35, pp. 156-8.

46. *ND*, N. 41, p. 87.

47. *Ibid.*, N. 45, p. 88.

48. *AS*, N. 29-30, pp. 156-7.

49. *EG*, N. 31, p. 269.

50. *Ibid.*, N. 35, p. 270. Different types of articulation with the non-theological (which are the pre-supposition and theme of theology) produce theological deviations such as the 'theology of becoming perfect in Christ' in India which 'did not take into account the universal poverty in India' (*ND*, N. 58, p. 93); the 'Ashram' movement which was incapable of passing beyond the level of personal ethics to the macroeconomic and structural level' (*ibid.*); or a theology of 'inculturation' which 'does not realise that they (these theologies) themselves identify with the culture of a particular class' (*ibid.*).

51. *BC*, N. 77, p. 244.

52. No one has done so much work on a theology of liberation with respect to the theologies of the periphery as James Cone. In his monumental *Black Theology: A Documentary History*, in collaboration with Gayraud Wilmore (Orbis, New York 1979), he dedicates the whole of part IV (pp. 445ff) to dialogues of theologies from peripheral countries: with theology in Africa, pp. 463ff; with Latin American liberation theology, pp. 510ff; with Marxist thought (pp. 543ff). The difference between the 'Black theology' of a central country and an 'African theology' which is not a theology of liberation can be observed in J. Mbiti 'An African views American Black Theology' (*ibid.* pp. 477-482). James Cone's contributions to our meetings were outstanding. See, by the same author, *My Soul Looks Back* (Abingdon, Nashville, 1982) pp. 93ff. (James' personal criticisms of my position I believe now to be in the past, cleared up since the appearance of Cornel West's works. See *National Cath. Reporter* XIX, 2 February (1983) p. 43, col. 1).

53. Since the start made in 1969, the Black Church of the US and the All Africa Conference Churches, in the central-peripheral relationship of a US minority with Africa, succeeded in holding their first meeting in Dar-es-Salaam, from 22nd to 28th August 1971 on 'Black Faith and Black Solidarity' (ed. P. Massie Friendship Press, New York 1973); see *Black Theology: a Documentary History*, Doc. 42, pp. 463ff. Thereafter another meeting was held in the Union Theological Seminary in New York, from 7th to 9th June 1973, at which differences appeared between the Black Theology of liberation of the centre and some African non-liberation theologies. This confrontation was more clearly apparent at the Accra Meeting (Ghana) from 29th to 31st December 1974. However some contradictions were also on the way towards being resolved. The results were published in *The Journal of Religious Thought*, XXXII, N. 2 (1975). We should also recall the meeting organised by EATWOT-Latin America in Kingston (Jamaica) in December 1979 in preparation for the Sao Paulo meeting (see my article which appeared, in part, in *Concilium* 151 (1982) pp. 54ff. 'A report on the situation in Latin America'. See *Black Theology: A Documentary History*, pp. 447-450 and pp. 477ff.

54. See *Fe cristiana y cambio social en America latina* (Sigueme, Salamanca 1973). (There are editions in English, French and Italian). In August 1972 the Escorial Meeting took place.

55. See *Theology in the Americas* (Orbis, New York 1976). 'Theology in the Americas II' is available through a photocopying service (Orbis, New York 1982). These meetings, organised by Sergio Torres, had the merit of launching various levels of liberation theology in the US.

56. See P. Freire, H. Assmann, E. Bodipo-Malumba, J. Cone *Teologia negra teologia de la liberacion* (Sigueme, Salamanca 1974). (The only complete publication of the meeting.) See also *Risk* IX, 2 (1973).

57. *Ibid.*, p. 135.

58. See *Praxi cristiana y produccion teologica* (Sigueme, Salamanca 1979). (Partial text in English in *Foundations* (Arlington), XXIII, 4 (1980). At this highly useful meeting, there were present, among others, J. Moltmann, H. Cox, J. Cone, D. Griffin, R. Vidales, H. Assmann, E. Dussel, O. Costas, etc. Various theologies confronted one another including the theology of hope, 'process theology', Black theology, liberation theology, etc.

59. See the 'Final Document' of the meeting in *Black Theology: A Documentary History* pp. 543-51.

60. *Ibid.*, p. 547.

61. *EG*, N. 31 (p. 269).

Contributors

JOSEPH A. BRACKEN, professor of theology at Xavier University in Cincinnati, Ohio, USA, completed doctoral studies in philosophy under the direction of Eugen Fink at the University of Freiburg, West Germany, in 1968. Subsequently, he taught at Saint Mary of the Lake Seminary in Mundelein, Illinois, and at Marquette University in Milwaukee, Wisconsin, before becoming chairman of the theology department at Xavier. He is the author of *Freiheit und Kausalität bei Schelling* (*Symposion*, n. 38: Freiburg i. Br., 1972) and of *What Are They Saying about the Trinity?* (New York 1979). Likewise, he has published scholarly articles in the *Heythrop Journal, Journal of the History of Philosophy, New Scholasticism, Process Studies* and *Theological Studies*.

ENRIQUE DUSSEL was born in Argentina in 1934. He holds a doctorate in philosophy and history from the Sorbonne. He is at present teaching at the autonomous university of Mexico. He is president of the Commission of Studies on the Church in Latin America (CEHILA), and has taken part in meetings of the Ecumenical Association of Third World Theologians in Dar-es-Salaam, Accra, Sri Lanka, Sao Paulo, New Delhi and Geneva. Of his many important works, those most recently translated into English are: *Ethic and Theology of Liberation* (1978) and *History of the Church in Latin America* (1980).

PETER EICHER was born in Winterthau, Switzerland in 1943. He studied philosophy, literature, history and theology in Freiburg and Tübingen. He is now Professor of Systematic Theology at the University of Paderborn. He is married, with 5 children. His publications include *Die anthropologische Wende* (1970); *Solidarischer Glaube* (1975); *Offenbarung—Prinzip neuzeitlicher Theologie* (1977); *Im Verborgenen offenbar* (1978); *Gottesvorstellung und Gesellschaftsentwicklung* (ed.) (1979); *Derr Herr gibts den Seinen im Schlaf* (1980); *Theologie. Eine Einführung in das Studium* (1980)—*La théologie comme science pratique* (1982); *Das Evangelium des Friedens* (ed.) (1982); *Bürgerliche Religion, Eine theologische Kritik* (1983).

VIRGIL ELIZONDO, Ph.D., S.T.D., was born in San Antonio, Texas (USA), studied at the Ateneo University (Manila), at the East Asian Pastoral Institute (Manila), and at the Institut Catholique (Paris). Since 1971 he has been president of the Mexican American Cultural Center in San Antonio. He has published numerous books and articles; been on the editorial board of *Concilium*, Catequesis Latino Americana and of the *God With Us Catechetical Series* (Sadlier Publishers, Inc. USA). He does much theological reflection with the grass-roots people in the poor neighbourhoods of the USA.

ELISABETH SCHÜSSLER FIORENZA has a licentiate in pastoral theology and a doctorate in New Testament Studies. She is currently professor of theology and NT Studies at the University of Notre Dame, Indiana. She has published numerous books and articles on New Testament Studies and Feminist Theology. She is active in the women's liberation movement in the Church and the academy and has served on various Task Forces on 'Women in the Church', 'Women in the Bible', or 'Women in Theology'. She was a member of the Core Commission of the Women's Ordination Conference, and together with Prof. Dr. Judith Plaskow is the founding editor of the *Journal of Feminist Studies in Religion.* Her most recent book is *In Memory of Her. A Feminist Theological Reconstruction of Christian Origins* (New York).

GUSTAVO GUTIÉRREZ was born in Lima, Peru, in 1928, and studied psychology at Louvain and theology at Lyons. He is National Assesor of the National Union of Catholic Students in Peru, and lectures in Theology and Social Science at the Catholic University of Lima. He is an editorial director of *Concilium.* His major translated work is *A Theology of Liberation*, published in Spanish in 1971, in English in 1973, which did much to bring this theology to the attention of the English-speaking world.

MEINRAD HEGBA was born in Cameroun. After studying for the priesthood he obtained a doctorate in philosophy from the Sorbonne, and also holds degrees in literature and social sciences. He has taught theology and anthropology at Jesuit universities in the United States and at the Gregorian University in Rome, and is now at the West African Catholic Institute in Abidjan, where he is engaged in research into witchcraft and exercises a ministry of healing by prayer in several West African countries.

His publications include, in addition to numerous articles, *Les Étapes des regroupements africains* (1968), *Croyance et guérison* (in collaboration, 1973), *Sorcellerie et Prière de Délivrance* (1982).

ERNST KÄSEMANN was born in 1906, in Bochum-Dahlhausen, Westphalia, Germany. He studied Protestant theology in Bonn, Marburg and Tübingen, taking his doctorate under R. Bultmann in 1931. After some years of parish work, he became professor for New Testament in Mainz (1946), Göttingen (1951), and then Tübingen (1959). He retired in 1971. He has honorary degrees from Marburg, Durham, Edinburgh and Oslo. Books translated into English are: *Essays on New Testament Themes* (1964); *New Testament Questions of Today* (1969); *The Testament of Jesus* (1968); *Jesus Means Freedom* (1969); *Perspectives on Paul* (1971); *Commentary on Romans* (1980). Latest publication: *Kirchliche Konflikte* (1982). He is the editor of *Das Neue Testament als Kanon* (1970).

NICHOLAS LASH was born in India in 1934. A Roman Catholic, he has been, since 1978, Norris-Hulse Professor of Divinity in the University of Cambridge. His publications include: *His Presence in the World* (1968); *Change in Focus* (1973); *Newman on Development* (1975); *Voices of Authority* (1976); *Theology on Dover Beach* (1979); and *A Matter of Hope: A Theologian's Reflections on the Thought of Karl Marx* (1981).

JOHANN-BAPTIST METZ, born at Welluck, near Auerbach, Bavaria, in 1928, was ordained a priest in 1954. He studied at the universities of Innsbruck and Munich and gained doctorates of philosophy and theology. He is professor of fundamental theology at the university of Münster and one of those responsible for setting up the university of Bielefeld. His works include: *Christliche Anthropozentrik* (1962); *Zur Theologie der Welt* (1968); *Reform und Gegenreformation heute* (1969); *Kirche im Prozess der Aufklärung* (1970); *Die Theologie in der interdisziplinären Forschung* (1971); *Leidensgeschichte* (1973); *Unsere Hoffnung* (1975); *Zeit der Orden? Zur Mystik und Politik der Nachfolge* (1977); *Glaube in Geschichte und Gesellschaft* (1977); *Jenseits bürgerlicher Religion* (1980); *Unterbrechungen* (1981).

JEAN-MARIE TILLARD, OP, was born in 1927 at Saint Pierre et Miquelon (France). He became a Dominican in 1950 and studied at Rome (philosophy) and Le Saulchoir in Paris. He was at the Second Vatican Council as an expert. Since then, he has been teaching in the Dominican Faculty at Ottawa and has been actively involved in ecumenical questions, serving on the Anglican-Catholic Commission ARCIC and the Orthodox-Catholic Commission Faith and Constitution as vice-president. His works, most of which have an ecumenical emphasis, include: *L'Eucharistie Pâque de l'Eglise* (1974); *Il y a charisme et charisme* (1977); *L'Évêque de Rome* (1982) and many contributions to *Irénikon, Lumen Vitae, Nouvelle Revue Théologique, Proche-Orient Chrétien, One in Christ* and *Midway*.

CONCILIUM 1983

NEW RELIGIOUS MOVEMENTS

Edited by John Coleman and Gregory Baum   161

LITURGY: A CREATIVE TRADITION

Edited by Mary Collins and David Power   162

MARTYRDOM TODAY

Edited by Johannes-Baptist Metz and
Edward Schillebeeckx   163

CHURCH AND PEACE

Edited by Virgil Elizondo and Norbert Greinacher   164

INDIFFERENCE TO RELIGION

Edited by Claude Geffré and Jean-Pierre Jossua   165

THEOLOGY AND COSMOLOGY

Edited by David Tracy and Nicholas Lash   166

THE ECUMENICAL COUNCIL AND THE CHURCH CONSTITUTION

Edited by Peter Huizing and Knut Walf   167

MARY IN THE CHURCHES

Edited by Hans Küng and Jürgen Moltmann   168

JOB AND THE SILENCE OF GOD

Edited by Christian Duquoc and Casiano Floristán   169

TWENTY YEARS OF CONCILIUM— RETROSPECT AND PROSPECT

Edited by Edward Schillebeeckx, Paul Brand and
Anton Weiler   170

All back issues are still in print: available from bookshops (price £3.50) or direct
from the publisher (£3.85/US$7.45/Can$8.55 including postage and packing).

T. & T. CLARK LTD, 36 GEORGE STREET, EDINBURGH EH2 2LQ, SCOTLAND

CONCILIUM

All back issues are still in print: available from bookshops (price £3.50) or direct from the publisher (£3.85/US$7.45/Can$8.55 including postage and packing).

T. & T. CLARK LIMITED
36 George Street, Edinburgh EH2 2LQ, Scotland

GOD is NEW EACH MOMENT

Edward Schillebeeckx

IN CONVERSATION WITH
HUUB OOSTERHUIS & PIET HOOGEVEEN

An encounter with Edward Schillebeeckx the human face
behind the great theologian. In response to the questions of
his colleagues, he provides a fascinating and comprehensive overview of his intellectual development and the
implications of the major themes of his work. The
discussions cover a wide range of topics including his ideas
about Jesus, the ministry and sacraments, the Scriptures,
the Church's future, the feminist movement and the
liberation of the poor.

'The interviewers take him through every phase of his life
and work and elicit from him replies of remarkable interest
and honesty. This book affords us valuable insights into the
mind and writings of a truly great theologian.'

Doctrine and Life

'. . . lets the reader much closer to the man: he is very open
and generous about his life and work; spontaneous, candid
and lively in his reactions to the questions. It also brings out
in a very natural way just how simple and deeply rooted Fr.
Schillebeeckx's faith remains.'
The Tablet

144 pages £3.95 paperback

T. & T. CLARK LTD, 36 GEORGE STREET, EDINBURGH EH2 2LQ, SCOTLAND